BREAKFAST IN·BED

California Cookbook

THE BEST B&B RECIPES FROM CALIFORNIA

Carol Frieberg

SASQUATCH BOOKS

SEATTLE

Printed in the United States of America.
Distributed in Canada by Raincoast Books Ltd.
01 99 98 97   5 4 3 2 1

Cover design: Karen Schober
Cover photograph: Angie Norwood Browne
Interior design and composition: Kate Basart
Interior illustrations: Jonathan Combs

Library of Congress Cataloging in Publication Data
Frieberg, Carol, 1959-
Breakfast in Bed California cookbook : the best B&B recipes
from California / Carol Frieberg.
p. cm.
Includes index.
ISBN 1-57061-107-6
1. Breakfasts. 2. Bed and breakfast accommodations—California. I. Title.
TX733.F75 1997
641.5'2—dc21   97-23538

SASQUATCH BOOKS
615 Second Avenue
Seattle, Washington 98104
(206) 467-4300
books@sasquatchbooks.com
http://www.sasquatchbooks.com

*Sasquatch Books publishes high-quality adult nonfiction and children's books
related to the Northwest (Alaska to San Francisco). For more information about our titles,
contact us at the address above, or view our site on the World Wide Web.*

To my family and friends who tested and tasted, offering
love and support in such good measure.
—C. F.

Contents

Scones & Muffins

Cinnamon-Glazed Scones	5
Cranberry Buttermilk Scones	7
Cherry Orange Scones	9
Date Pecan Scones	11
Oatmeal Scones	13
Gingerbread Muffins	15
Super Cinnamon Muffins	17
Mini Lemon Muffins	19
Ginger-Pear Muffins	21
Apricot Cornmeal Muffins	23
Apple-Cranberry Muffins	25
Pumpkin Pie Muffins	27
Mandarin Orange Muffins	29
Cran-Blackberry Muffins	31
Mini Cake Doughnut Muffins	33

Breads & Coffee Cakes

Eye-Opener Jalepeño Corn Bread	37
English Muffin Bread	39
Irish Soda Bread	41
Hawaiian Bread	43
Pecan Pumpkin Bread	45
Strawberry Nut Bread	47

Tart Lemon Tea Bread   49

Low-Fat Pineapple Bread   51

Raspberry Cream Cheese Coffee Cake   53

Pumpkin Cranberry Coffee Cake   55

Sour Cream Coffee Cake   57

Apple Coffee Cake   59

Spiced Banana Cake   61

Chocolate Zucchini Rum Cake   63

Blueberry Cream Cheese Coffee Cake   65

Applesauce Cake   67

Plum Coffee Cake   69

Fresh Rhubarb Cake   71

White Fruit Cake   73

House Specialties

Breakfast Muesli   77

Crunchy Nut Granola   79

Homestead Granola   81

Apple Oatmeal Crisp   83

Fresh Cherry Cobbler   85

Summer Plum Pie   87

Pear Dutch Baby   89

Breakfast Berry Pudding   91

Apple Pie Bread Pudding   93

Banana Nut Bread Pudding   95

Fresh Fig Baked Custard   97

Cinnamon Raisin Breakfast Custard   99

Cottage Cheese Blintz   101

Oatmeal and Cranberry Soufflé   103

Decadent French Toast Soufflé   105

Cheese Blintz Soufflé   107

Cinnamon Rolls   109

Espresso Biscotti   111

Walnut Shortbread   113

Mimosa Truffles   115

Pancakes, Waffles & French Toast

Oatmeal Buttermilk Pancakes   119

Fluffy Blueberry Pancakes   121

German Apple Pancakes   123

Ricotta Pancakes   125

Apple Walnut Pancakes   127

Orange Thyme Pancakes   129

Apfel Pfannkuchen   131

Apple Oven-Baked Pancake   133

Seasonal Fruit Crepes   135

Hazelnut Waffles with Peaches   137

Cornmeal and Oat Waffles   139

Pumpkin Spice Waffles   141

Whole Wheat Belgian Waffles   143

Rum Custard French Toast   145

Caramel Apple French Toast 147

Peach-Stuffed French Toast 149

Sunday's Baked French Toast 151

Lemon-Poppy Seed French Toast 153

Pineapple French Toast 155

Portuguese French Toast 157

Apple-Pecan French Toast 159

Breakfast Egg Dishes

Italian Morning Eggs 163

Eggs Madison 165

Chiles Rellenos 167

Herbed Baked Eggs 169

Creamy Eggs with Caviar 171

Mock Eggs Benedict 173

Victorian Eggs 175

Crab Soufflé 177

Mini Cheese Soufflés 179

Cornmeal Soufflé 181

Mayan Maize Tortilla Pie 183

Italian Zucchini Frittata 185

Hash Brown Quiche 187

Spinach Mushroom Quiche 189

Vegetarian Crustless Quiche 191

Ham and Cheese Breakfast Pie 193

Green Chile and Potato Tart 195

Eggs for a Crowd

Bella Torta   199

Cheesy Potato Pie   201

Eggs for a Gang   203

Sausage Strata   205

Artichoke Mushroom Strata   207

Sonoma County Egg Casserole   209

Baked Sour Cream Omelet   211

Italian Sausage Frittata   213

Artichoke Frittata   215

Eggs Gruyère with Savory Garnish   217

Hash Brown Casserole   219

Fruit, Sides & Sauces

La Belle Grapes with Rosemary   223

Baked Banana Crumble   225

Broiled Blackberries   227

Peaches and Cream   229

Poached Pears in Raspberry Sauce   231

Morning Baked Apples   233

Warm Berry Sauce   235

Gala Orange Sauce   237

Lemon Curd   239

Date-Nut Butter   241

Maricela's Salsa   243

Basil Tomatoes with Pine Nuts   245

Baked Breakfast Polenta   247

Sausage with Grapes   249

German Potato Pancakes   251

Rosemary Roasted Potatoes   253

Ballard Home-Fried Potatoes   255

Bed and Breakfast Inns   257

Index   266

Introduction

reakfast in bed! The very sound of it conjures up feelings of indulgence, pampering, and celebration. My grandmother understood this very well. When I was a little girl, she served my brother and me French toast in bed on Sunday mornings. My appreciation was further developed when I managed a bed and breakfast in Door County, Wisconsin. Whether it is sitting down to a gourmet country breakfast or simply having a mug of freshly brewed coffee brought to you in bed, the beauty lies in taking something ordinary and turning it into something special.

Whether you're an avid bed-and-breakfast traveler or someone who just loves to cook, the recipes in this book will expand your breakfast horizons. Each recipe has been chosen from select California bed-and-breakfast establishments and reflects the distinctive character of each region and inn. Recipes use fresh local ingredients, are surprisingly easy to prepare, and many can be made ahead of time.

So let the recipes in *Breakfast in Bed California Cookbook* bring the simple elegance of a bed and breakfast into your home. From Raspberry Cream Cheese Coffee Cake to Chiles Rellenos, these recipes will help you create a memorable breakfast (in or out of bed!).

Here's to mornings worth savoring!

—Carol Frieberg

Scones
& Muffins

Cinnamon
Glazed
Scones

CINNAMON BEAR BED & BREAKFAST
St. Helena, California

2 cups all-purpose flour

¼ cup granulated sugar

1 tablespoon baking powder

½ teaspoon salt

½ cup golden raisins

¼ cup raisins

1¼ cups heavy (whipping) cream

GLAZE:

3 tablespoons butter, melted

Cinnamon sugar (1½ tablespoons granulated sugar mixed with 1 tablespoon ground cinnamon)

Preheat oven to 400°F. In large bowl, combine flour, sugar, baking powder, and salt; stir in raisins. Add cream until mixture clings together and forms soft dough. Turn dough onto lightly floured surface and knead gently 10 times. Pat dough into a ½-inch-thick circle. Cut with biscuit or heart-shaped cookie cutter. (*Note:* Scones can be frozen at this point.) Place on baking sheet lined with parchment paper. Brush scones lightly with melted butter and sprinkle with cinnamon sugar mixture. Bake about 15 minutes or until golden.

Twenty scones

Cranberry
Buttermilk
Scones

JOSHUA GRINDLE INN
Mendocino, California

1½ cup cold butter	1 cup dried cranberries
4 cups all-purpose flour	1 cup sliced almonds, toasted
½ cup granulated sugar	1 egg, lightly beaten
4 teaspoons baking powder	1½ cups buttermilk
1 teaspoon baking soda	2 teaspoons almond extract
1 teaspoon salt	

*P*reheat oven to 425°F. In large bowl, cut butter into flour, sugar, baking powder, baking soda, and salt until mixture resembles fine crumbs. Stir in dried cranberries and almonds. Add egg, buttermilk, and almond extract; mix until mixture clings together and forms soft dough. Turn dough onto lightly floured surface and knead gently about 15 times. Divide dough equally into quarters and pat into ½-inch-thick circles. Cut each circle into 6 wedges. Place on lightly greased baking sheets. Brush scones lightly with buttermilk and sprinkle with granulated sugar and a few sliced almonds if desired. Bake 12 to 15 minutes or until golden brown. Serve warm.

Twenty-four scones

Cherry
Orange
Scones

THE HONOR MANSION
Healdsburg, California

6 tablespoons cold butter

2 cups all-purpose flour

2 tablespoons granulated sugar

1 tablespoon baking powder

½ teaspoon salt

1 tablespoon finely grated orange rind

¾ cup dried cherries

1 egg, lightly beaten

½ cup milk

GLAZE:

1 cup powdered sugar

1 to 2 tablespoons orange juice

1 teaspoon finely grated orange rind

Preheat oven to 400°F. In large bowl, cut butter into flour, sugar, baking powder, and salt until mixture resembles fine crumbs. Stir in orange rind and dried cherries. Add egg and milk; mix until mixture clings together and forms soft dough. Turn dough onto lightly floured surface and knead gently about 15 times. Divide dough into fourths and pat into squares about ½ inch thick. Cut each square diagonally twice to form 4 triangles. Place on lightly greased baking sheet (or freeze for future baking). Bake about 15 minutes or until lightly browned. In small bowl, combine powdered sugar, orange juice, and orange rind to desired consistency. Spoon glaze over hot scones; let cool 5 minutes. Serve warm.

Sixteen scones

Date
Pecan
Scones

HARTLEY HOUSE BED & BREAKFAST INN
Sacramento, California

4 tablespoons cold butter

2⅓ cups all-purpose flour

3 tablespoons brown sugar

1 tablespoon baking powder

½ teaspoon baking soda

½ teaspoon salt

½ cup chopped pitted dates

½ cup chopped pecans

1 egg, lightly beaten

¾ cup heavy (whipping) cream

1 teaspoon vanilla extract

*P*reheat oven to 400°F. In large bowl, cut butter into flour, brown sugar, baking powder, baking soda, and salt until mixture resembles fine crumbs. Stir in dates and pecans. Add egg, cream, and vanilla; mix until mixture clings together and forms soft dough. Turn dough onto lightly floured surface and knead gently about 30 seconds. Pat dough into ¾-inch-thick circle. Cut into 8 wedges. Place on ungreased baking sheet. Brush scones lightly with cream and sprinkle with granulated sugar if desired. Bake 15 to 18 minutes or until golden.

Eight scones

Oatmeal
Scones

THE GEORGE ALEXANDER HOUSE
Healdsburg, California

½ cup cold butter

1¼ cups all-purpose flour

⅓ cup brown sugar

1 teaspoon baking powder

½ teaspoon baking soda

½ teaspoon salt

1 cup old-fashioned oats

⅓ cup golden raisins

⅓ cup buttermilk

*P*reheat oven to 375°F. In large bowl (or food processor), cut butter into flour, sugar, baking powder, baking soda, and salt until mixture resembles fine crumbs; stir in oats and raisins. Add buttermilk and mix until mixture clings together and forms soft dough. Turn dough onto lightly floured surface and pat into a 7-inch circle. Cut into 8 wedges. Place on ungreased baking sheet. Bake 12 to 15 minutes or until golden. Cool slightly.

Eight scones

Gingerbread
Muffins

THE CARRIAGE HOUSE
Laguna Beach, California

½ cup shortening	2 teaspoons ground ginger
½ cup margarine	½ teaspoon ground cinnamon
1 cup granulated sugar	½ teaspoon ground cloves
1 cup dark molasses	½ teaspoon ground allspice
4 eggs	1 cup sour cream
2 teaspoons baking soda	1 cup raisins
1 cup buttermilk	1 cup chopped pecans, toasted
4 cups all-purpose flour	

*P*reheat oven to 350°F. In large bowl, cream shortening, margarine, sugar, and molasses. Add eggs, one at a time, beating well after each. In small bowl, dissolve baking soda in buttermilk. In separate bowl, combine flour and spices. Add flour mixture alternately with buttermilk to creamed mixture. Fold in sour cream, raisins, and pecans. Fill greased muffin cups two-thirds full. Bake 20 to 25 minutes or until muffins test done. *Note:* This batter can be stored in covered airtight container in refrigerator up to two weeks.

Twenty-four muffins

Super
Cinnamon
Muffins

ABIGAIL'S BED & BREAKFAST
Sacramento, California

2 eggs	*2 teaspoons baking powder*
1 cup milk	*2 tablespoons ground cinnamon*
½ cup vegetable oil	*¼ teaspoon salt*
1 cup brown sugar	*1 cup chopped walnuts or pecans*
2 cups all-purpose flour	*1 cup raisins*

*P*reheat oven to 375°F. In large bowl, beat eggs, milk, oil, and brown sugar. Stir in flour, baking powder, cinnamon, and salt; mix just until blended. Fold in walnuts and raisins. Fill greased muffin cups two-thirds full. Bake 15 to 20 minutes or until muffins test done.

Twelve muffins

Mini
Lemon
Muffins

MEADOW CREEK RANCH BED & BREAKFAST
Mariposa, California

½ cup butter, softened   1 cup all-purpose flour

½ cup granulated sugar   1 teaspoon baking powder

Grated rind of 1 lemon   ¼ teaspoon salt

2 eggs, separated   ¼ cup lemon juice

Preheat oven to 400°F. In large bowl, cream butter, sugar, and lemon rind. Add egg yolks and beat well. In separate bowl, combine flour, baking powder, and salt. Add flour mixture alternately with lemon juice to creamed mixture, mixing well after each addition. In separate bowl, beat egg whites until stiff; fold into batter. Fill greased mini muffin cups two-thirds full. Bake 12 to 15 minutes or until lightly browned.

Eighteen mini muffins

Ginger-Pear
Muffins

COAST GUARD HOUSE HISTORIC INN
Point Arena, California

2 eggs	½ teaspoon ground cardamom
2 teaspoons milk	1 tablespoon finely chopped
½ cup vegetable oil	crystallized ginger
¾ cup granulated sugar	2 medium pears, peeled, cored,
2 cups all-purpose flour	and finely chopped
2 teaspoons baking powder	¾ cup chopped walnuts
½ teaspoon salt	½ cup raisins

Preheat oven to 350°F. In large bowl, beat eggs, milk, oil, and sugar. Stir in flour, baking powder, salt, cardamom, and crystallized ginger; mix just until blended. Fold in pears, walnuts, and raisins. Fill greased muffin cups two-thirds full. Bake 20 to 25 minutes or until muffins test done. Cool briefly on wire rack. Best served warm.

Twelve muffins

Apricot
Cornmeal
Muffins

COLUMBIA CITY HOTEL
Columbia, California

1¼ cups butter, softened	5 cups all-purpose flour
2 cups granulated sugar	1 cup cornmeal
5 eggs	1½ tablespoons baking powder
1 teaspoon vanilla extract	1½ tablespoons baking soda
4 cups buttermilk	3 cups finely chopped dried apricots

*P*reheat oven to 350°F. In large bowl, cream butter and sugar with electric mixer; add eggs and vanilla. With mixer running slowly, add buttermilk (do not overmix). Add flour, cornmeal, baking powder, and baking soda; mix just until combined (batter will be lumpy). Fold in dried apricots. Fill greased muffin cups two-thirds full. Bake 20 to 25 minutes or until muffins test done.

Thirty muffins

Apple-Cranberry Muffins

CAPTAIN'S COVE INN
Mendocino, California

2 eggs

1 cup milk

½ cup vegetable oil

1 cup granulated sugar

3 cups all-purpose flour

4 teaspoons baking powder

1 teaspoon salt

1½ teaspoons ground cinnamon

1 cup dried cranberries

½ cup golden raisins

2 small cooking apples, peeled, cored, and chopped

Cinnamon sugar (¼ cup granulated sugar mixed with ¾ teaspoon ground cinnamon)

Preheat oven to 400°F. In large bowl, beat eggs, milk, oil, and sugar. Stir in flour, baking powder, salt, and cinnamon; mix just until blended (batter will be thick). Fold in dried cranberries, raisins, and apples. Fill greased muffin cups two-thirds full. Sprinkle with cinnamon sugar mixture. Bake 20 to 25 minutes or until muffins test done.

Twelve muffins

Pumpkin
Pie
Muffins

THE ZABALLA HOUSE BED & BREAKFAST
Half Moon Bay, California

2 eggs	¾ cup brown sugar
¼ cup buttermilk	1½ teaspoons baking powder
½ cup butter, melted	¼ teaspoon baking soda
3 tablespoons molasses	¾ cup coarsely chopped
¾ cup canned pumpkin	pecans or walnuts
1 teaspoon vanilla extract	¾ cup chopped pitted dates
2 cups all purpose flour	

Preheat oven to 400°F. In large bowl, beat eggs, buttermilk, butter, molasses, pumpkin, and vanilla. Stir in flour, brown sugar, baking powder, and baking soda; mix just until blended. Fold in pecans and dates. Fill greased muffin cups two-thirds full. Bake 20 to 25 minutes or until muffins test done. Cool 5 minutes before transferring muffins to wire rack.

Twelve muffins

Mandarin
Orange
Muffins

ORCHARD HILL COUNTRY INN
Julian, California

1 can (11 ounces) mandarin orange
segments

1 tablespoon orange extract

1 egg

1 cup sour cream

½ cup unsalted butter, melted

½ cup granulated sugar

½ cup brown sugar

2 cups all-purpose flour

2 teaspoons baking powder

½ teaspoon baking soda

½ teaspoon salt

½ cup chopped pecans

Preheat oven to 400°F. Drain oranges; reserve liquid. Cut oranges in half and place in measuring cup. Add orange extract and reserved liquid to equal 1 cup. In large bowl, beat egg, sour cream, butter, and sugars; stir in orange mixture. Add flour, baking powder, baking soda, and salt; mix just until blended. Fold in pecans. Fill greased muffin cups two-thirds full. Bake 20 to 25 minutes or until muffins test done.

Twelve muffins

Cran-Blackberry
Muffins

THE DALY INN
Eureka, California

1 egg	1 teaspoon salt
¾ cup milk	1 tablespoon grated lemon peel
½ cup vegetable oil	¾ cup fresh or frozen blackberries
⅓ cup granulated sugar	½ cup chopped fresh or frozen
2 cups all-purpose flour	cranberries
1 tablespoon baking powder	½ cup chopped hazelnuts

Preheat oven to 400°F. In large bowl, beat egg, milk, oil, and sugar. Stir in flour, baking powder, salt, and lemon peel; mix just until blended. Fold in blackberries, cranberries, and hazelnuts. Fill greased muffin cups two-thirds full. Bake about 20 minutes or until muffins test done.

Twelve muffins

Mini Cake
Doughnut
Muffins

TRES PALMAS BED & BREAKFAST
Palm Desert, California

1 egg

½ cup milk

⅓ cup butter or margarine, melted

½ cup granulated sugar

½ teaspoon vanilla extract

1½ cups all-purpose flour

2 teaspoons baking powder

¼ teaspoon salt

¼ teaspoon ground nutmeg

3 tablespoons butter, melted

Cinnamon sugar (⅓ cup granulated
  sugar mixed with ½ teaspoon
  ground cinnamon)

Preheat oven to 350°F. In large bowl, beat egg, milk, ⅓ cup melted butter, sugar, and vanilla. Stir in flour, baking powder, salt, and nutmeg; mix just until blended. Spoon into greased mini muffin cups. Bake about 15 minutes or until golden. While warm, brush doughnut tops with the 3 tablespoons melted butter and roll in cinnamon sugar mixture. Serve warm or cool.

Twenty-four mini muffins

Breads
& Coffee Cakes

Eye-Opener
Jalepeño
Corn Bread

MENDOCINO VILLAGE INN
Mendocino, California

1 cup buttermilk	1 teaspoon baking powder
1 cup cornmeal	½ teaspoon baking soda
¼ cup corn oil	1 can (8 ounces) creamed corn
2 eggs	1 can (4 ounces) diced jalapeños
1 cup all-purpose flour	1 cup shredded Cheddar cheese
3 tablespoons granulated sugar	¼ cup shredded Monterey jack cheese

Preheat oven to 375°F. In large bowl, combine buttermilk and cornmeal; let stand 30 minutes. Stir in remaining ingredients; mix well. Pour into greased 13-by-9-inch baking pan. Bake about 30 minutes or until bread tests done.

One loaf

English
Muffin
Bread

PRUFROCK'S GARDEN INN

Carpinteria, California

6 cups all-purpose flour, divided

2 packages active dry yeast

1 tablespoon granulated sugar

2 teaspoons salt

¼ teaspoon baking soda

2 cups milk

½ cup water

Cornmeal

In large bowl, combine 3 cups flour, yeast, sugar, salt, and baking soda. Heat milk and water to 120°F and add to dry mixture; mix well. Gradually stir in remaining flour. Divide batter into two greased 9-by-5-inch loaf pans that have been dusted with cornmeal. Sprinkle loaves lightly with cornmeal. Cover loaves with warm clean cloth and let rise in warm place for about 30 minutes. Preheat oven to 400°F. Bake about 25 minutes or until loaves are golden brown and sound hollow when tapped. Remove from pans; cool on wire rack.

Two loaves

Irish
Soda
Bread

J. PATRICK HOUSE BED & BREAKFAST
Cambria, California

1 cup butter or margarine	2 cups sour cream
6 tablespoons granulated sugar	1 cup raisins
4 cups all-purpose flour	2 tablespoons caraway seeds
1½ teaspoons baking soda	Milk
1 teaspoon salt	

*P*reheat oven to 350°F. In large bowl, cream butter and sugar. Add flour, baking soda, and salt; beat on low speed until crumbly. Stir in sour cream, raisins, and caraway seeds until mixture clings together and forms soft dough. Turn dough onto lightly floured surface and knead about 30 seconds. Divide dough in half and place on greased baking sheet. Pat each into a smooth flat round loaf. Brush loaves lightly with milk. Bake 50 to 60 minutes or until golden brown.

Two loaves

Hawaiian
Bread

SILVER ROSE INN & SPA
Calistoga, California

3 eggs	1 teaspoon ground cinnamon
1 cup vegetable oil	1 can (8 ounces) crushed pineapple,
2 cups granulated sugar	drained
2 teaspoons vanilla extract	1 cup grated coconut
2½ cups all-purpose flour	2 cups raw grated carrots
1 teaspoon baking soda	

*P*reheat oven to 350°F. In large bowl, beat eggs, oil, sugar, and vanilla. Stir in flour, baking soda, and cinnamon; mix just until blended. Fold in pineapple, coconut, and carrots. Divide batter evenly into two greased 9-by-5-inch loaf pans and let rest 20 minutes. Bake about 1 hour or until bread tests done. Cool completely (bread cuts better next day).

Two loaves

Pecan
Pumpkin
Bread

VINEYARD COUNTRY INN
St. Helena, California

2 eggs	½ teaspoon baking powder
⅓ cup water	½ teaspoon salt
½ cup vegetable oil	½ teaspoon ground cinnamon
1½ cups sugar	½ teaspoon ground nutmeg
1 cup canned pumpkin	½ teaspoon ground allspice
1¾ cups all-purpose flour	⅔ cup chopped pecans
1 teaspoon baking soda	½ cup chopped pitted dates

*P*reheat oven to 350°F. In large bowl, beat eggs, water, oil, sugar, and pumpkin. Stir in flour, baking soda, baking powder, salt, and spices; mix just until blended. Fold in pecans and dates. Pour into greased 9-by-5-inch loaf pan. Bake about 1 hour or until bread tests done. Cool completely (bread slices better next day).

One loaf

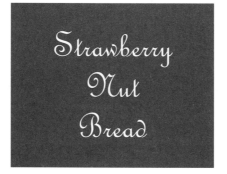

Strawberry
Nut
Bread

THE INN SAN FRANCISCO
San Francisco, California

2 eggs	½ teaspoon baking soda
½ cup vegetable oil	½ teaspoon salt
1 cup granulated sugar	1 cup milk
½ teaspoon vanilla extract	½ cup finely chopped walnuts
1½ cups all-purpose flour	¾ cup chopped fresh strawberries

*P*reheat oven to 350°F. In large bowl, beat eggs, oil, sugar, and vanilla. In separate bowl, combine flour, baking soda, and salt. Add flour mixture alternately with milk to creamed mixture. Fold in walnuts and strawberries. Pour into greased 9-by-5-inch loaf pan. Bake about 1 hour or until bread tests done.

One loaf

Tart
Lemon Tea
Bread

INN AT PLAYA DEL REY
Playa del Rey, California

¾ cup butter, softened	2 tablespoons grated lemon rind
2 cups granulated sugar	⅓ cup lemon juice
4 eggs	3 cups all-purpose flour
¾ cup sour cream	2 teaspoons baking powder
½ cup milk	1 cup fresh raspberries

Preheat oven to 325°F. Cream butter and sugar; add eggs, sour cream, milk, lemon rind, and lemon juice. Stir in flour and baking powder; mix just until blended. Fold in raspberries. Pour batter into greased 10-inch bundt pan. Bake about 1 hour or until cake tests done. Cool before slicing.

Sixteen servings

Low-Fat
Pineapple
Bread

BEAZLEY HOUSE
Napa, California

3 eggs	1 can (20 ounces) crushed pineapple,
1 cup buttermilk	drained
2 tablespoons vegetable oil	4½ cups all-purpose flour
2 cups granulated sugar	3 teaspoons baking soda
2 teaspoons vanilla extract	1 teaspoon baking powder
1 cup applesauce	½ teaspoon ground cinnamon

Preheat oven to 325°F. In large bowl, beat eggs, buttermilk, oil, sugar, and vanilla. Stir in applesauce and pineapple; mix well. Stir in flour, baking soda, baking powder, and cinnamon; mix just until blended. Spray 10-inch bundt pan with nonstick cooking spray. Pour batter into pan. Bake about 45 minutes or until bread tests done.

Twenty servings

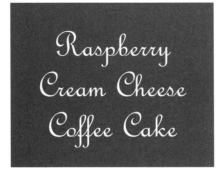

Raspberry
Cream Cheese
Coffee Cake

CAMPBELL RANCH INN
Geyserville, California

2½ cups all-purpose flour

¾ cup granulated sugar

¾ cup cold butter

½ teaspoon baking powder

½ teaspoon baking soda

¼ teaspoon salt

¾ cup sour cream

1 egg, lightly beaten

1 teaspoon almond extract

FILLING:

8 ounces cream cheese

¼ cup granulated sugar

1 egg, lightly beaten

½ cup raspberry jam

TOPPING:

½ cup sliced almonds

Preheat oven to 350°F. In large bowl, combine flour and ¾ cup sugar; cut in butter until mixture resembles coarse crumbs. Remove 1 cup of crumbs for topping; reserve. To remaining crumb mixture, add baking powder, baking soda, salt, sour cream, egg, and almond extract; mix well. Spread batter in greased and floured 9-inch springform pan. In small bowl, combine cream cheese, ¼ cup sugar, and egg; spread evenly over batter in pan. Spoon jam evenly over the cheese filling. Combine reserved crumbs with almonds; sprinkle over top. Bake 1 hour or until cream cheese is set and crust is deep golden brown. Cool 15 minutes; remove sides of pan and cool completely. Serve warm or at room temperature.

Twelve servings

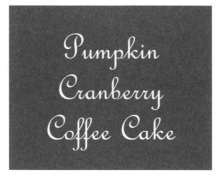

Pumpkin
Cranberry
Coffee Cake

THE CHICHESTER-MCKEE HOUSE
Placerville, California

2 eggs	1 teaspoon baking soda
½ cup vegetable oil	½ teaspoon salt
2 cups granulated sugar	1 tablespoon pumpkin pie spice
1 cup canned pumpkin	1 cup chopped fresh cranberries
2¼ cups all-purpose flour	

*P*reheat oven to 350°F. In large bowl, beat eggs, oil, sugar, and pumpkin. Stir in flour, baking soda, salt, and pumpkin pie spice; mix just until combined. Fold in cranberries. Spread batter evenly in greased 8-cup ring mold. Place mold on baking sheet. Bake about 50 minutes or until cake tests done. Cool mold on wire rack 10 minutes. Run knife around edge of cake to loosen and remove from mold. Dust with powdered sugar, if desired.

Twelve servings

Sour
Cream
Coffee Cake

1 cup butter, softened	1 tablespoon baking powder
2 cups granulated sugar	¼ teaspoon salt
2 eggs	
2 cups sour cream	FILLING:
1 tablespoon vanilla extract	2 cups finely chopped pecans
1 cup whole wheat flour	½ cup granulated sugar
1 cup all-purpose flour	1½ teaspoons ground cinnamon

*P*reheat oven to 350°F. In large bowl, cream butter and sugar; add eggs, sour cream, and vanilla. Stir in flours, baking powder, and salt; mix well. Pour half of batter into greased and floured 10-inch bundt pan. Combine filling ingredients, sprinkle half of filling over batter. Top with remaining batter and sprinkle with remaining filling mixture. Bake about 1 hour or until cake tests done.

Twelve servings

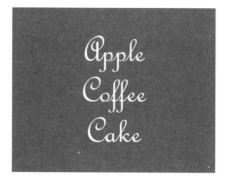

Apple
Coffee
Cake

VICHY HOT SPRINGS RESORT & INN
Ukiah, California

¼ cup butter, softened

1 cup granulated sugar

3 eggs

1 teaspoon vanilla extract

2½ cups all-purpose flour

1 tablespoon baking powder

1 teaspoon salt

1 cup milk

5 cooking apples, peeled, cored, and grated

Cinnamon sugar (2 tablespoons granulated sugar mixed with ½ teaspoon ground cinnamon)

TOPPING:

2 tablespoons cold butter

½ cup granulated sugar

½ cup all-purpose flour

GLAZE:

1¼ cups powdered sugar

2 tablespoons milk

Preheat oven to 350°F. In large bowl, cream butter and sugar; add eggs and vanilla. In separate bowl, combine flour, baking powder, and salt. Add flour mixture alternately with milk to butter mixture. Spread batter in greased 15-by-10-inch baking pan. Sprinkle grated apples over batter. Sprinkle lightly with cinnamon sugar mixture. In medium bowl, cut butter into sugar and flour until mixture resembles fine crumbs; sprinkle over apples. Bake about 40 minutes or until cake tests done. In small bowl, blend powdered sugar with milk; glaze cake while still warm.

Sixteen servings

Spiced
Banana
Cake

⅔ cup butter, softened

2⅔ cups granulated sugar

4 eggs

½ cup water

4 large bananas, mashed

3⅓ cups all-purpose flour

2 teaspoons baking powder

2 teaspoons baking soda

4 teaspoons ground cinnamon

½ teaspoon ground nutmeg

½ teaspoon ground cloves

1 cup finely chopped walnuts

Cinnamon sugar (2 tablespoons granulated sugar mixed with ½ teaspoon
ground cinnamon)

Preheat oven to 325°F. In large bowl, cream butter and sugar; add eggs, water, and bananas. Stir in flour, baking powder, baking soda, cinnamon, nutmeg, and cloves; mix well. Spread batter in greased 10-inch bundt pan. Sprinkle with walnuts and cinnamon sugar mixture. Bake about 1 hour or until cake tests done.

Sixteen servings

Chocolate
Zucchini
Rum Cake

¾ cup butter, softened

2 cups granulated sugar

3 eggs

2 cups lightly packed shredded zucchini

⅓ cup rum, brandy, or water

¼ cup milk

2½ cups all-purpose flour

½ cup unsweetened cocoa

2½ teaspoons baking powder

1½ teaspoons baking soda

1 teaspoon salt

¾ teaspoon ground cinnamon

1 cup chopped walnuts

GLAZE:

1⅔ cups powdered sugar

3 tablespoons rum or water

*P*reheat oven to 350°F. In large bowl, beat butter and sugar with electric mixer until smooth. Beat in eggs, one at a time, until fluffy. Stir in zucchini, rum, and milk. Add flour, cocoa, baking powder, baking soda, salt, and cinnamon; mix well. Fold in walnuts. Spread batter in greased and floured 10-inch bundt pan. Bake 50 to 55 minutes or until cake springs back when firmly pressed in center. Let cool in pan 15 minutes. Invert onto rack and let cool. Mix powdered sugar and rum; drizzle over cake.

Sixteen servings

Blueberry
Cream Cheese
Coffee Cake

APPLE LANE INN
Aptos, California

1½ cups granulated sugar	1½ cups frozen blueberries
3 cups all-purpose flour	3 eggs
4 teaspoons baking powder	½ cup sour cream
1 teaspoon salt	⅔ cup milk
8 ounces cream cheese, cut into	½ cup butter, melted
½-inch cubes	1 cup chopped walnuts

Preheat oven to 350°F. In large bowl, combine sugar, flour, baking powder, and salt. Toss cream cheese and blueberries into flour mixture to coat. In separate bowl, beat eggs, sour cream, milk, and butter. Stir milk mixture into dry ingredients; mix just until combined. Spread batter in greased 13-by-9-inch baking pan; sprinkle with walnuts. Bake 55 to 60 minutes or until cake tests done.

Sixteen servings

Applesauce
Cake

BAYVIEW HOTEL, A COUNTRY INN
Aptos, California

¾ cup raisins	½ teaspoon ground cinnamon
⅓ cup cream sherry or apple juice	½ teaspoon ground allspice
2 eggs	¼ teaspoon ground cloves
½ cup vegetable oil	¼ teaspoon ground nutmeg
1½ cups brown sugar	2 teaspoons baking soda
1½ cups applesauce	¾ cup chopped walnuts
2½ cups all-purpose flour	

Preheat oven to 350°F. In small saucepan, heat raisins and cream sherry to boiling; remove from heat and set aside. In large bowl, beat eggs, oil, and brown sugar. Stir in applesauce, flour, and spices; mix well. Stir baking soda into raisin and sherry mixture; stir into batter. Fold in walnuts. Pour batter into greased 10-inch bundt pan. Bake about 45 minutes or until cake tests done.

Sixteen servings

Plum
Coffee
Cake

OLD THYME INN
Half Moon Bay, California

2 eggs	TOPPING:
1 cup milk	6 tablespoons butter
½ cup vegetable oil	1 cup brown sugar
1½ cups granulated sugar	6 tablespoons all-purpose flour
3 cups all-purpose flour	1½ teaspoons ground cinnamon
1 tablespoon baking powder	1 cup chopped walnuts
1 teaspoon salt	
6 to 8 plums, pitted and sliced	

*P*reheat oven to 350°F. In large bowl, beat eggs, milk, oil, and sugar. Stir in flour, baking powder, and salt; mix well. Spread batter in greased and floured 13-by-9-inch glass baking dish. Top with rows of plum slices. In medium bowl, combine topping ingredients; mix until crumbly and sprinkle over plums. Bake about 1 hour or until cake tests done.

Eighteen servings

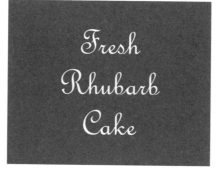

Fresh
Rhubarb
Cake

THE PALM HOTEL BED & BREAKFAST
Jamestown, California

½ cup butter, softened

1 cup brown sugar

1 egg

1 teaspoon vanilla extract

2 cups all-purpose flour

1 teaspoon baking soda

½ teaspoon salt

1 cup buttermilk

2 cups fresh rhubarb, cut into
¼-inch pieces

TOPPING:

2 tablespoons butter, melted

½ cup brown sugar

1 teaspoon ground cinnamon

½ cup chopped walnuts or almonds

*P*reheat oven to 350°F. In large bowl, cream butter and brown sugar; add egg and vanilla. In separate bowl, mix flour, baking soda, and salt. Add dry ingredients to creamed mixture alternately with buttermilk. Fold in rhubarb. Pour into greased 13-by-9-inch baking pan. Mix topping; sprinkle evenly over batter. Bake 45 to 50 minutes or until cake tests done.

Twelve servings

White
Fruit
Cake

RYAN HOUSE, 1855
Sonora, California

¾ cup butter, softened

1¼ cups granulated sugar

½ teaspoon vanilla extract

½ teaspoon orange extract

2 eggs, lightly beaten

¾ cup buttermilk or sour milk

2½ cups all purpose flour

½ teaspoon baking soda

¼ teaspoon salt

1 cup grated coconut

2 cups golden raisins

1 cup candied mixed peels

½ cup chopped dried apricots

½ cup diced orange peel

Blanched whole almonds

Preheat oven to 300°F. In large bowl, cream butter and sugar; add vanilla and orange extracts, eggs, and buttermilk. In separate bowl, combine all remaining ingredients except almonds; toss until fruits are well coated. Stir flour mixture into creamed mixture; mix well. Spread batter in greased and floured 10-inch bundt pan. Decorate with blanched almonds. Bake 2 hours or until cake tests done. Cool cake in pan on wire rack. (Cake may be wrapped in cloth soaked in brandy or bourbon and wrapped in foil if desired.)

Sixteen servings

House
Specialties

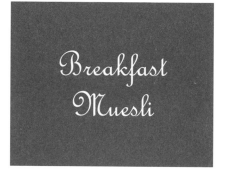

Breakfast Muesli

THE PHILO POTTERY INN
Philo, California

9 large shredded wheat biscuits,
crumbled

3 cups old-fashioned oats

1 cup wheat bran

1 cup wheat germ

¼ cup brown sugar

¾ cup raisins, dried cherries,
or dried cranberries

¾ cup dried apricots, diced

½ cup sliced almonds

*I*n large bowl, combine all ingredients; mix well. Store in airtight container. Serve with milk or yogurt and fresh fruit if desired.

Ten cups

Crunchy
Nut
Granola

6 cups old-fashioned oats

¾ cup broken cashews

¾ cup broken pecans

¾ cup pine nuts

½ cup nut or vegetable oil

½ cup orange blossom honey

⅓ cup hot water

1½ teaspoons vanilla extract

¾ cup dried fruit (golden raisins, dried cherries)

Preheat oven to 325°F. In large bowl, combine oats and nuts. In separate bowl, whisk together oil, honey, hot water, and vanilla. Add honey mixture to dry ingredients; mix well. Transfer mixture to greased jelly roll pan. Bake about 40 minutes, stirring frequently, until golden brown. Remove from oven; cool. Stir in dried fruit. Store in airtight container.

Eight cups

Homestead
Granola

HOMESTEAD BED & BREAKFAST
Julian, California

8 cups old-fashioned oats ½ cup vegetable oil

1½ cups brown sugar ½ cup honey

2 cups sliced almonds ½ cup water

1½ cups shaved coconut (not grated)

Preheat oven to 325°F. In large bowl, combine oats, brown sugar, almonds, and coconut. In small saucepan, heat oil, honey, and water just until boiling. Pour honey mixture over dry ingredients; mix well. Divide evenly between 2 greased 13-by-9-inch baking pans. Bake about 1 hour, stirring every 20 minutes, until golden brown; cool. Store in air-tight container.

Twelve cups

Apple
Oatmeal
Crisp

SUTTER CREEK INN
Sutter Creek, California

4 cups peeled and thinly sliced tart
cooking apples

1½ tablespoons fresh lemon juice

3½ tablespoons granulated sugar

⅓ cup all-purpose flour

1 cup old-fashioned oats

½ cup brown sugar

1 teaspoon ground cinnamon

½ teaspoon salt

½ cup butter, melted

*P*reheat oven to 375°F. Combine apples, lemon juice, and granulated sugar in greased 9-inch-square baking pan. In separate bowl, combine remaining ingredients; spoon evenly over apples. Bake 35 minutes or until topping is golden and apples are tender.

Six servings

Fresh
Cherry
Cobbler

ROCKWOOD GARDENS BED & BREAKFAST
Mariposa, California

1¼ cups granulated sugar	*1 tablespoon granulated sugar*
3 tablespoons cornstarch	*1½ teaspoons baking powder*
4 cups fresh, pitted sweet cherries	*½ teaspoon salt*
¼ teaspoon almond extract	*3 tablespoons shortening*
1 cup all-purpose flour	*½ cup milk*

Preheat oven to 400°F. Mix 1¼ cups sugar and cornstarch in medium saucepan. Add cherries and almond extract. Cook over medium heat, stirring constantly, until mixture thickens and comes to a boil. Boil and stir 1 minute. Pour into ungreased 8-inch-square baking pan. Keep fruit mixture hot in oven while preparing biscuit topping. In large bowl, mix flour, 1 tablespoon sugar, baking powder, and salt. Cut in shortening until mixture looks like fine crumbs. Stir in milk; mix until dough forms ball. Drop dough by 9 spoonfuls onto hot fruit. Bake 25 minutes or until topping is golden brown. Serve warm with whipped topping or cream if desired.

Nine servings

Summer
Plum
Pie

SERENITY BED & BREAKFAST INN
Sonora, California

PASTRY:	FILLING:
1 cup all-purpose flour	*8 plums, pitted and cut into*
⅓ cup granulated sugar	*½-inch slices*
½ cup butter, softened	*¼ cup water*
	⅓ cup all-purpose flour
	¾ cup granulated sugar
	¼ teaspoon baking powder
	1 egg, slightly beaten

Preheat oven to 350°F. In medium bowl, combine flour and ⅓ cup sugar. Cut in butter until crumbly. Press into 9-inch pie plate. Bake about 20 minutes or until golden. Increase oven temperature to 375°F. In medium skillet, heat plums and water over medium heat until juice thickens slightly; remove from heat. In large bowl, combine flour, ¾ cup sugar, baking powder, egg, and enough juice from plums to form smooth batter. Stir plums into batter; mix until evenly coated. Pour into cooled crust. Bake 20 to 25 minutes; cool.

Eight servings

Pear
Dutch
Baby.

GLENELLY INN
Glen Ellen, California

2 tablespoons butter	*1 to 2 ripe pears, peeled or unpeeled*
5 eggs	*Juice of 1 lemon*
½ cup milk or cream	*Powdered sugar*
½ cup all-purpose flour	

Preheat oven to 450°F. Melt butter in 9-inch nonstick skillet. Pour half of butter into medium bowl. Beat eggs into butter. Add milk and flour; mix well. Slice pears and sauté briefly in reserved butter in skillet. Drizzle pears with lemon juice and sprinkle lightly with powdered sugar. Arrange pears in pretty pattern in bottom of skillet. Pour egg mixture over pears. (Wrap skillet handle with foil if not oven-proof.) Bake 20 to 25 minutes or until puffy and golden. Invert onto serving platter. Dust with powdered sugar. Serve immediately.

Four servings

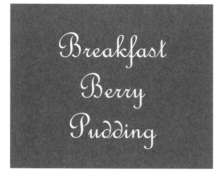

Breakfast
Berry
Pudding

BLUE SPRUCE INN
Soquel, California

4 slices day-old white bread

3 to 4 ounces cream cheese

Cinnamon sugar (1 tablespoon

granulated sugar mixed with ¼

teaspoon ground cinnamon)

1 cup fresh raspberries or blueberries

¼ cup brown sugar, divided

1 tablespoon butter, diced

4 eggs

1 cup milk

1 teaspoon vanilla extract

*P*reheat oven to 350°F. Spread each slice bread with cream cheese and sprinkle with cinnamon sugar mixture. Cube bread and place in bottom of greased 8-inch-square baking pan. Distribute berries evenly over bread. Sprinkle half the brown sugar and all the butter over cubes. Beat together eggs, milk, and vanilla; pour over cubes. Sprinkle with remaining brown sugar. Set pan in larger shallow pan; add 1 inch hot water after pan has been placed on oven rack. Bake 35 to 40 minutes or until knife inserted in center comes out clean. Cool pudding before cutting into squares. Serve in pool of fresh berry sauce and top with dollop of sour cream if desired.

Four servings

Apple Pie
Bread
Pudding

MURPHY'S INN
Grass Valley, California

1 loaf French bread, cut into
1-inch cubes
8 eggs
8 ounces cream cheese
3 cups buttermilk
¼ cup granulated sugar
1 tablespoon vanilla extract

¼ teaspoon salt
1 can (21 ounces) cinnamon and spice
apple pie filling
Cinnamon sugar (2 tablespoons
granulated sugar mixed with
½ teaspoon ground cinnamon)

Distribute bread cubes evenly in greased 13-by-9-inch baking pan. In large bowl, beat eggs, cream cheese, buttermilk, sugar, vanilla, and salt. Stir in pie filling; mix well. Pour buttermilk mixture over bread cubes. Sprinkle lightly with cinnamon sugar mixture. Cover and refrigerate overnight. Remove from refrigerator. Preheat oven to 350°F. Uncover and bake 45 to 60 minutes or until puffed and golden brown. Let stand 5 minutes before serving.

Twelve servings

Banana Nut
Bread
Pudding

ANDERSON CREEK INN
Boonville, California

1 large loaf banana nut bread

2 ripe bananas, thinly sliced

12 eggs

2 cups milk

½ cup chopped walnuts

½ teaspoon ground cinnamon

3 tablespoons granulated sugar

CREAM SAUCE:

1 cup milk

½ cup butter

¼ cup granulated sugar

Preheat oven to 325°F. Cut banana bread into cubes and place in greased 13-by-9-inch baking pan. Toss bread cubes with banana slices; distribute evenly in pan. In large bowl, beat eggs and milk. Pour egg mixture over bread and bananas. In small bowl, mix walnuts, cinnamon, and sugar; sprinkle over bread mixture. Bake 1 hour or until toothpick comes out clean. Let set 5 to 10 minutes before cutting. In medium saucepan, bring milk, butter, and sugar to boil. Boil about 5 minutes, stirring constantly, until froth settles down and sugar is dissolved. Remove from heat; allow to cool slightly. Serve pudding with warm cream sauce.

Ten servings

Fresh Fig
Baked
Custard

ADOBE INN
San Luis Obispo, California

1 cup granulated sugar	1 teaspoon vanilla extract
6 tablespoons all-purpose flour	1 teaspoon bourbon or rum
2½ teaspoons baking powder	1 cup chopped pecans or walnuts
Pinch salt	1 cup diced and stemmed fresh figs
2 eggs	1 teaspoon grated fresh lemon rind

*P*reheat oven to 350°F. In large bowl, mix sugar, flour, baking powder, and salt. In separate bowl, beat eggs, vanilla, and bourbon; stir into dry ingredients. Fold in pecans, figs, and lemon rind. Mix several minutes or until well blended. Pour into greased 8-inch-square baking pan. Bake 30 to 35 minutes or until knife inserted in middle comes out clean; cool. Cover and refrigerate overnight. Serve with cream or fresh whipped cream if desired.

Nine servings

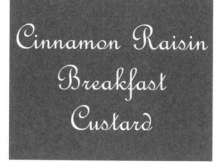

Cinnamon Raisin
Breakfast
Custard

THE WHALE WATCH INN
Gualala, California

1 loaf sliced cinnamon raisin bread,
crusts removed
½ cup butter, melted
7 eggs plus 3 egg yolks

¾ cup granulated sugar
1 cup heavy (whipping) cream
3 cups milk

Preheat oven to 350°F. Layer bread in 13-by-9-inch baking pan. Pour melted butter evenly over bread. In large bowl, beat eggs, egg yolks, sugar, cream, and milk; pour evenly over bread. Place pan in larger pan of hot water. Bake 1 hour or until custard is set. Let stand 20 minutes before cutting. Sprinkle with powdered sugar if desired. *Note:* This dish can be assembled the night before.

Eight servings

Cottage
Cheese
Blintz

JOSHUA TREE INN BED & BREAKFAST
Joshua Tree, California

¼ cup cottage cheese	3 tablespoons sour cream
2 teaspoons granulated sugar	2 tablespoons all-purpose flour
2 tablespoons butter	Finely chopped walnuts
1 egg	Granulated sugar

*I*n small bowl, combine cottage cheese and sugar; set aside. In 8-inch skillet, melt butter. In separate bowl, beat egg, sour cream, and flour. Pour batter into skillet and cook pancake-style, turning when bubbles form on surface and edges become puffed and dry. Spoon cottage cheese mixture onto one half of pancake; fold over other half (a little mixture may melt in with butter in pan and can be used as sauce). Cook until golden brown. Sprinkle lightly with walnuts and granulated sugar. Serve with fresh berries if desired.

One serving

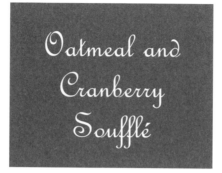

Oatmeal and
Cranberry
Soufflé

2 tablespoons butter	2 tablespoons grated orange peel
1½ cups nonfat milk	3 tablespoons Grand Marnier or
1½ cups quick-cooking oats	orange juice concentrate
4 ounces light cream cheese	4 egg yolks
¾ cup brown sugar	1 cup dried cranberries
1½ teaspoons ground cinnamon	¾ cup chopped pecans or walnuts,
1 teaspoon ground nutmeg	toasted
½ teaspoon salt	5 egg whites

*P*reheat oven to 325°F. In large saucepan, heat butter and milk until butter is melted. Add oats; stir until thick. Remove from heat. Add cream cheese, brown sugar, cinnamon, nutmeg, salt, orange peel, Grand Marnier, and egg yolks; mix well. In separate bowl, beat egg whites until stiff; fold into oat mixture until almost smooth (don't overfold). Fold in dried cranberries and pecans. Pour into greased 1½-quart soufflé dish. Bake 40 to 45 minutes or until edges are set (center will still tremble). *Note:* This can also be baked in 6 large ramekins or custard cups for 30 to 35 minutes.

Six servings

Decadent
French Toast
Soufflé

FOOTHILL HOUSE BED AND BREAKFAST
Calistoga, California

4 large or 5 medium croissants (baked)

8 ounces cream cheese, softened

½ cup butter, softened

¾ cup maple syrup, divided

10 eggs

3 cups half-and-half

1 teaspoon ground cinnamon

Powdered sugar

Chopped pecans

SAUCE:

½ cup butter

½ cup maple syrup

In food processor, coarsely chop croissants; distribute evenly in greased 13-by-9-inch casserole dish. In food processor, combine cream cheese, butter, and ¼ cup maple syrup; spread evenly over chopped croissants. In large bowl, beat eggs, ½ cup maple syrup, and half-and-half; pour over mixture. Sprinkle with cinnamon. Cover and refrigerate overnight. Remove from refrigerator. Preheat oven to 350°F. Uncover and bake 45 to 50 minutes or until golden. In small saucepan, heat ½ cup butter and ½ cup maple syrup; pour over warm soufflé. Sprinkle with powdered sugar and chopped pecans.

Eight servings

Cheese
Blintz
Soufflé

MELITTA STATION INN
Santa Rosa, California

3 tablespoons butter or margarine,
melted

1 box (13 ounces) frozen cheese blintzes

4 eggs

1¼ cups sour cream

¼ cup orange juice

½ cup granulated sugar

2 teaspoons vanilla extract

Dash salt

*P*our butter into 11-by-7-inch glass baking dish. Place blintzes in dish in single layer. In medium bowl, beat remaining ingredients; pour over frozen blintzes. Cover and refrigerate overnight. Remove from refrigerator. Preheat oven to 350°F. Uncover and bake 45 to 55 minutes or until puffed and golden.

Six servings

Cinnamon
Rolls

2 packages active dry yeast

2½ cups lukewarm water (120°
to 130°F)

1 box (1 pound, 2.25 ounces) yellow
cake mix

5½ cups all-purpose flour

½ cup butter, melted

1 cup granulated sugar

1 tablespoon ground cinnamon

GLAZE:

2 cups powdered sugar

1 teaspoon vanilla extract

3 to 4 tablespoons milk

*I*n large bowl, dissolve yeast in water. Stir in cake mix and flour; mix or knead until smooth and elastic. Cover and let rise in a warm place until double. Punch down dough. Roll out dough into ½-inch-thick rectangle, about 15 by 20 inches. Spread butter evenly over dough. Mix sugar and cinnamon; sprinkle over dough. Roll dough into a log and cut into 1-inch slices. Place in 2 greased 13-by-9-inch baking pans (rolls will be touching). Cover and refrigerate overnight. Remove from refrigerator. Preheat oven to 350°F. Uncover and bake 30 to 35 minutes or until golden brown. Cool slightly. To make glaze, combine ingredients and stir until smooth and of drizzling consistency. Drizzle glaze over rolls. Rolls best served warm.

Twenty rolls

Espresso
Biscotti

AGATE COVE INN BED & BREAKFAST
Mendocino, California

1 egg	½ teaspoon baking soda
4 teaspoons milk	½ teaspoon salt
¼ cup plus 1 tablespoon espresso	½ teaspoon ground cinnamon
or strong coffee	¼ teaspoon ground cloves
1 cup granulated sugar	¾ cup mini chocolate chips
1 teaspoon vanilla extract	(semi-sweet)
2 cups all-purpose flour	¾ cup finely chopped walnuts
½ teaspoon baking powder	¾ cup dried cranberries or cherries

Preheat oven to 350°F. In large mixing bowl, beat egg, milk, espresso, sugar, and vanilla. Stir in flour, baking powder, baking soda, salt, and spices; mix well. Fold in chocolate chips, walnuts, and dried cranberries. Place dough onto greased and floured baking sheet. Pat into ½-inch-thick rectangle, about 12 by 4 inches. Bake 20 to 25 minutes or until toothpick inserted in center comes out clean. Cool 15 minutes. Decrease oven temperature to 300°F. Cut logs crosswise into ½-inch slices. Place slices cut-side down on baking sheet. Bake 15 minutes, turning once. Cool on wire rack.

Twenty-four servings

Walnut
Shortbread

RACHEL'S INN
Mendocino, California

1 cup all-purpose flour   ½ cup butter, cut into small pieces
½ cup granulated sugar   ½ cup chopped walnuts

*P*reheat oven to 350°F. In food processor, pulse together flour, sugar, and butter just until mixed. Add walnuts and pulse until chopped (butter and flour should resemble coarse crumbs). Pat mixture firmly into a 9-inch springform pan. Bake 25 to 30 minutes or until golden brown. Remove from oven and immediately release and remove sides of pan. Cut shortbread into 16 wedges (do not remove from bottom of pan until completely cool).

Sixteen servings

Mimosa
Truffles

INN ON SUMMER HILL
Summerland, California

10 ounces bittersweet chocolate
1 cup powdered sugar, divided
2 egg yolks
½ cup heavy (whipping) cream

¼ cup butter
1 ounce Grand Marnier
2 ounces champagne
Cocoa powder

Melt chocolate in double boiler or microwave; set aside. In large bowl, beat ½ cup powdered sugar and egg yolks. In saucepan or double boiler, bring cream, ½ cup powdered sugar, and butter to boil, stirring constantly; cool slightly. Whisk cream mixture into yolk mixture. Gradually add melted chocolate, Grand Marnier, and champagne; stir until well blended. Refrigerate 4 hours or until set. Roll into balls, 1 inch in diameter. Roll balls in cocoa powder. Keep refrigerated.

Forty truffles

Pancakes, Waffles & French Toast

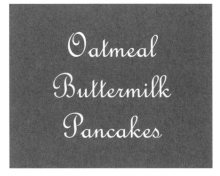

Oatmeal
Buttermilk
Pancakes

LOST WHALE INN
Trinidad, California

2 cups buttermilk	2 tablespoons granulated sugar
2 cups old-fashioned oats	1 teaspoon baking powder
2 eggs, lightly beaten	1 teaspoon baking soda
¼ cup butter, melted	¼ teaspoon salt
1 teaspoon vanilla extract	½ teaspoon ground cinnamon
½ cup all-purpose flour	½ cup currants

In large bowl, combine buttermilk and oats; let soak ½ hour or overnight. Add remaining ingredients; mix well. Heat griddle or skillet over medium heat and grease if necessary. Pour ¼ cup batter onto hot griddle. Cook pancakes until puffed and dry around edges. Turn and cook on other side until golden brown.

Fourteen pancakes

Fluffy
Blueberry
Pancakes

WHITE HORSE INN BED & BREAKFAST
Mammoth Lakes, California

1 egg	*1 teaspoon baking powder*
½ cup plain yogurt	*1 teaspoon baking soda*
½ cup milk	*¼ teaspoon salt*
2 tablespoons vegetable oil	*⅛ teaspoon ground nutmeg*
1 cup all-purpose flour	*¾ cup fresh or frozen blueberries*
1 tablespoon granulated sugar	

In large bowl, beat egg, yogurt, milk, and oil. Stir in flour, sugar, baking powder, baking soda, salt, and nutmeg; mix just until blended (batter may be slightly lumpy). Heat griddle or skillet over medium heat and grease if necessary. Pour ¼ cup batter onto hot griddle. Sprinkle pancakes with blueberries. Turn when bubbles form on surface. Cook on other side until golden brown. Serve warm with butter and maple syrup if desired.

Twelve pancakes

German
Apple
Pancakes

MCCLOUD RIVER INN
McCloud, California

---

2 eggs   ¼ teaspoon salt

⅔ cup apple juice   3 medium apples, peeled,

½ cup water   cored, and grated

1½ cups all-purpose flour

In medium bowl, beat eggs, apple juice, water, flour, and salt. Stir in apples; mix until smooth. Heat griddle or skillet over medium heat and grease if necessary. Drop about 3 tablespoons batter onto hot griddle and spread thinly with back of spoon. Cook pancakes until puffed and dry around edges. Turn and cook other side until golden brown. Remove from skillet and keep warm in oven (set on low). Sprinkle with cinnamon sugar if desired.

Eight pancakes

Ricotta
Pancakes

THE GABLES BED & BREAKFAST INN
Santa Rosa, California

3 eggs, separated	½ cup all-purpose flour
1 cup ricotta cheese	1 teaspoon baking powder
⅔ cup milk	½ teaspoon salt

In large bowl, beat egg yolks, ricotta, milk, flour, baking powder, and salt. In separate bowl, beat egg whites until stiff. Gently fold egg whites into ricotta mixture. Heat griddle or skillet over medium heat and grease if necessary. Pour ¼ cup batter onto hot griddle. Cook pancakes until puffed and dry around edges. Turn and cook other side until golden brown. Serve with sour cream and jam or whipped cream and fresh berries if desired.

Sixteen pancakes

Apple
Walnut
Pancakes

THE GRAVENSTEIN INN
Sebastopol, California

2 eggs	½ teaspoon salt
2 tablespoons vegetable oil	1 teaspoon ground cinnamon
3 cups buttermilk	½ teaspoon ground mace
2 cups whole wheat pastry flour	½ cup chopped walnuts or hazelnuts
½ cup raw wheat germ	1 cooking apple (unpeeled), chopped
1 teaspoon baking soda	

In large bowl, beat eggs, oil, and buttermilk. Stir in remaining ingredients; mix just until blended. (If batter is too runny or too thick, adjust with buttermilk or flour as needed.) Heat griddle or skillet over medium heat and grease if necessary. Pour ¼ cup batter onto hot griddle. Cook until edges are dry; turn and cook other side until golden brown. Serve with maple syrup and plain yogurt if desired.

Sixteen pancakes

Orange
Thyme
Pancakes

THE INN AT OCCIDENTAL
Occidental, California

2 cups all-purpose flour

¼ cup granulated sugar

2 teaspoons baking soda

1 teaspoon salt

2 eggs, beaten

1¾ cups orange juice

¼ cup butter, melted

1 tablespoon chopped fresh thyme

ORANGE SAUCE:

½ cup butter, melted

3 tablespoons cornstarch

2 cups orange juice

⅔ cup granulated sugar

2 tablespoons orange zest

*I*n large bowl, combine dry ingredients. Add eggs, orange juice, butter, and thyme; mix just until blended. Heat griddle or skillet over medium heat and grease if necessary. Pour ¼ cup batter onto hot griddle. When bubbles appear on surface, turn and cook on other side until golden brown. To prepare orange sauce, heat butter and cornstarch over medium heat 1 minute. Add orange juice; stir until thickened. Add sugar and bring to boil. Reduce heat and simmer 5 minutes until sugar is dissolved. Stir in orange zest. Add an equal amount of maple syrup to orange sauce if desired.

Sixteen pancakes

Apfel
Pfannkuchen

BOULDER CREEK BED & BREAKFAST
Yosemite-Mariposa, California

5 eggs	1½ cups buttermilk pancake mix
½ cup water	Butter for frying
1 teaspoon vanilla extract	3 apples, peeled, cored, and thinly sliced
1 teaspoon ground cinnamon	

In large bowl, beat eggs, water, vanilla, and cinnamon until well blended. Add pancake mix; mix just until blended. Melt 2 tablespoons butter in skillet. Ladle batter to make 3-inch pancakes. Immediately place apple slices on top of batter to cover entire pancake. Cook pancakes until golden brown and bubbly. Turn pancakes (adding butter if necessary) and continue to cook until golden brown and crusty. Serve pancakes apple-side up. Serve with maple syrup if desired.

Sixteen pancakes

Apple
Oven-Baked
Pancake

THE SWEDISH HOUSE BED & BREAKFAST
Truckee, California

2 eggs	3 tablespoons granulated sugar, divided
1 cup milk	¼ teaspoon ground cinnamon
3 tablespoons melted butter	1½ Golden Delicious apples, peeled,
¾ cup all-purpose flour	cored, and thinly sliced
½ teaspoon salt	

Preheat oven to 425°F. In large bowl, beat eggs, milk, and butter. Stir in flour, salt, and 1 tablespoon sugar; mix well. Pour batter into greased 10-inch cast-iron skillet. Combine 1 tablespoon sugar with cinnamon; toss with apple slices. Arrange apple wedges on batter in pinwheel design. Bake 20 minutes. Reduce oven temperature to 350°F. Bake 10 minutes or until edges are puffed and center is set. Sprinkle with remaining tablespoon sugar. Serve immediately.

Two servings

Seasonal
Fruit
Crepes

INN ON TOMALES BAY
Marshall, California

2 eggs	Vanilla yogurt
½ cup low-fat milk	Fresh mint sprigs
½ cup water	Seasonal fruit (sliced peaches,
1 cup all-purpose flour	fresh raspberries)
¼ teaspoon salt	Raspberry sauce or syrup
Sliced banana	

In large bowl, beat eggs, milk, and water. Stir in flour and salt to make thin batter. Let batter rest in refrigerator 1 hour. Spray 7-inch skillet with nonstick cooking spray; heat over medium-high heat. Pour ⅛ cup batter into skillet; tilt pan to coat bottom evenly with a thin layer of batter. Cook crepe on one side only, just until it begins to curl away from sides of pan, 1 to 2 minutes. Slide crepe onto plate and repeat with remaining batter, spraying pan as needed. Stack crepes on top of one another; cool. To assemble crepes, place slices of banana down center of crepe; top with a few spoonfuls of yogurt. Fold each side of crepe over center. Place two crepes on plate. Garnish with dollop of yogurt and mint sprig. Surround with fresh fruit. Drizzle raspberry syrup in zigzag pattern over crepes. Lightly sift powdered sugar over entire plate if desired.

Twelve crepes

Hazelnut
Waffles
with Peaches

ALBION RIVER INN

Albion, California

1¼ cups milk

½ cup heavy (whipping) cream

¼ cup butter

¼ cup granulated sugar

Pinch salt

1¼ cups bread flour

1 tablespoon baking powder

3 eggs

¼ cup chopped hazelnuts

TOPPING:

½ cup vanilla yogurt

Sliced fresh peaches

In medium saucepan, heat milk, cream, butter, sugar, and salt over medium heat until butter is melted and sugar is dissolved; remove from stove. Pour milk mixture into large bowl. Add flour and baking powder all at once; stir vigorously. Beat in eggs, one at a time, using an electric mixer. Fold in hazelnuts. (If batter is too runny or too thick, adjust with milk or flour as needed.) Let stand 5 minutes. Heat waffle iron and grease if necessary. Bake in hot waffle iron until golden brown. Top with yogurt and peaches. Serve with warm maple syrup if desired.

Six 7-inch waffles

Cornmeal
and
Oat Waffles

CARRIAGE HOUSE BED & BREAKFAST
Point Reyes, California

---

2 eggs	½ cup stone-ground yellow cornmeal
1¾ cups buttermilk	½ cup old-fashioned oats
¼ cup butter, melted	2 teaspoons baking powder
1 cup all-purpose flour	

In large bowl, beat eggs, buttermilk, and butter. Add flour, cornmeal, oats, and baking powder; mix just until smooth (add a little more buttermilk to batter if too thick). Heat waffle iron and grease if necessary. Bake in hot waffle iron until golden brown. Serve with warm maple syrup if desired.

Six 7-inch waffles

Pumpkin
Spice
Waffles

3 eggs	2 teaspoons baking powder
1 cup milk	½ teaspoon salt
2 tablespoons butter, melted	¼ teaspoon ground nutmeg
2 tablespoons granulated sugar	¼ teaspoon ground cloves
½ cup canned pumpkin	¼ teaspoon ground cinnamon
1 cup all-purpose flour	

In large bowl, beat eggs, milk, butter, sugar, and pumpkin. Add flour, baking powder, salt, and spices; mix just until smooth. Heat waffle iron and grease if necessary. Bake in hot waffle iron until golden brown. Serve immediately with warm maple syrup, fresh berries, or whipped cream and a dusting of ground ginger if desired.

Six 4-inch waffles

141

Whole Wheat
Belgian
Waffles

4 eggs, separated	2½ teaspoons baking powder
1⅓ cups milk	¾ teaspoon baking soda
1 cup plain yogurt	½ teaspoon salt
⅓ cup vegetable oil	1½ cups cooked wild rice
2 tablespoons honey	1 cup chopped pecans, toasted
2 cups whole wheat flour	

*I*n large bowl, beat egg yolks, milk, yogurt, oil, and honey. Stir in flour, baking powder, baking soda, and salt; mix just until blended. In separate bowl, beat egg whites until stiff but not dry; gently fold into batter. Cook waffles according to directions for waffle iron. Pour scant cupful of batter into center of hot Belgian waffler. Sprinkle 3 tablespoons wild rice and 2 tablespoons pecan pieces over batter and bake until golden brown.

Eight 4-inch waffles

Rum
Custard
French Toast

EAST BROTHER LIGHT STATION
Point Richmond, California

12 slices French bread, 1 inch thick

Cinnamon sugar (2 tablespoons
granulated sugar mixed with ½
teaspoon ground cinnamon)

6 eggs plus 3 egg yolks

2½ cups milk

⅔ cup granulated sugar

⅓ cup dark rum

1 teaspoon vanilla extract

BUTTER-RUM SAUCE:

½ cup butter

1 cup powdered sugar

1 egg, lightly beaten

1 to 2 tablespoons dark rum

Preheat oven to 375°F. Dust each slice of bread with cinnamon sugar mixture. Cut bread in half diagonally and cut corners off. Arrange bread in greased 13-by-9-inch baking dish. In large bowl, beat eggs, egg yolks, milk, sugar, rum, and vanilla. Pour egg mixture over bread; let stand 5 minutes. Fill larger pan about one-third full with boiling water; set baking dish into pan. Bake 45 to 60 minutes or until puffy and golden brown. In small saucepan, melt butter; whisk in powdered sugar. Whisk in egg and rum and heat until thick. Serve warm sauce with French toast.

Eight servings

Caramel
Apple
French Toast

WHITEGATE INN BED & BREAKFAST
Mendocino, California

½ cup butter

1 cup brown sugar

2 tablespoons light corn syrup

1 cup chopped pecans

12 slices sweet French bread,

¾ inch thick

6 to 8 green apples, peeled, cored,

and thinly sliced

6 eggs

1½ cups milk

1 teaspoon vanilla extract

½ teaspoon ground cinnamon

⅛ teaspoon ground nutmeg

In small saucepan, heat butter, brown sugar, and corn syrup over medium heat; stir constantly until thickened. Spray 13-by-9-inch glass baking dish with nonstick cooking spray. Pour butter mixture into dish; sprinkle with pecans. Arrange 6 bread slices over pecans; top with apple slices. Combine remaining ingredients in blender; process until blended. Pour half of egg mixture over apples; top with second layer of bread. Pour remaining egg mixture over bread. Cover and refrigerate overnight. Preheat oven to 350°F. Bake uncovered 50 to 60 minutes or until golden brown. Serve with whipped cream if desired.

Six servings

Peach-Stuffed
French
Toast

PELICAN COVE INN
Carlsbad, California

10 to 12 slices white bread, crusts removed	FILLING:
3 eggs	8 ounces cream cheese
2 cups half-and-half	¼ cup granulated sugar
½ cup granulated sugar	1 egg
1 teaspoon vanilla extract	1 teaspoon vanilla extract
Dash ground nutmeg	1 can (16 ounces) peach halves, drained

*A*rrange half of bread in bottom of greased 11-by-7-inch glass baking dish. In medium bowl, beat eggs, half-and-half, sugar, and vanilla. Pour half of egg mixture over bread. In separate bowl, beat filling ingredients; pour evenly over bread mixture. Cut peach halves horizontally into ¼-inch slices; place over filling. Arrange remaining bread slices over peaches. Pour remaining egg mixture over bread. Sprinkle with nutmeg. Cover and refrigerate overnight. Preheat oven to 350°F. Cover and bake 30 minutes. Uncover and bake 30 to 40 minutes longer or until puffy and golden brown. Serve warm with maple syrup if desired.

Six servings

Sunday's
Baked
French Toast

APPLEWOOD INN
Guerneville, California

6 eggs	¼ teaspoon vanilla extract
⅔ cup orange juice	¼ teaspoon salt
⅓ cup Grand Marnier	8 slices day-old French bread,
⅓ cup heavy (whipping) cream	¾ inch thick
3 tablespoons granulated sugar	

In large bowl, beat eggs, orange juice, Grand Marnier, cream, sugar, vanilla, and salt. Dip bread slices into mixture, turning to coat both sides. Place bread slices in shallow dish; pour any remaining egg mixture over top. Cover and refrigerate overnight. Next day, heat griddle or skillet over medium heat and grease if necessary. Cook bread on hot griddle until golden brown on both sides. Top with fresh fruit or syrup if desired.

Four servings

Lemon
Poppy Seed
French Toast

SCOTT COURTYARD
Calistoga, California

12 eggs

1¼ cups milk

Juice and zest of ½ lemon

1½ tablespoons poppy seeds

12 slices French bread, ¾ inch thick

¼ cup butter

SYRUP:

1 cup maple syrup

¼ cup raisins

Juice and zest of ½ lemon

*I*n large bowl, beat eggs, milk, lemon juice, lemon zest, and poppy seeds; pour into large shallow pan. Soak bread slices in egg mixture 30 minutes, turning once. Heat griddle or skillet over medium heat. Cook bread in butter on hot griddle until golden brown on both sides. Heat maple syrup, raisins, lemon juice, and lemon zest over medium heat until warm. Serve syrup with French toast. Garnish with lemon slices if desired.

Six servings

Pineapple
French
Toast

BEN MADDOX HOUSE
Visalia, California

6 eggs

2 teaspoons vanilla extract

2 tablespoons sour cream

1 can (8 ounces) crushed pineapple, drained

½ cup half-and-half

2 tablespoons maple syrup

12 slices French bread, ¾ inch thick

In blender, combine eggs, vanilla, sour cream, pineapple, half-and-half, and syrup; blend until smooth. Place bread in large shallow pan; pour egg mixture over bread. Soak bread thoroughly, then turn to soak other side. Heat griddle or skillet over medium heat and grease if necessary. Cook bread on hot griddle until golden brown on both sides. Sprinkle with powdered sugar and garnish with canned pineapple slices if desired.

Six servings

Portuguese
French
Toast

MAYFIELD HOUSE BED & BREAKFAST
Tahoe City, California

1 can (29 ounces) sliced peaches, drained	*1 cup half-and-half*
¾ cup maple syrup	*Dash ground nutmeg*
6 eggs	*1 round loaf Hawaiian sweet bread*

In medium saucepan, bring peaches and maple syrup to boil. Reduce heat and simmer peaches 30 minutes. In medium bowl, beat eggs, half-and-half, and nutmeg. Pour egg mixture into shallow bowl. Cut bread loaf in half and slice each half into six 1-inch slices. Dip slices of bread into batter, turning to coat both sides. Heat griddle or skillet over medium heat and grease if necessary. Cook bread on hot griddle until golden brown on both sides. Transfer to platter and sprinkle with powdered sugar if desired. Serve with warm peaches and maple syrup.

Six servings

Apple-Pecan
French
Toast

ARBOR HOUSE INN
Lakeport, California

¼ cup butter

3 Granny Smith apples, peeled, cored, and sliced

½ cup granulated sugar

1 tablespoon ground cinnamon

5 eggs

¼ cup half-and-half

1 teaspoon vanilla extract

6 slices sweet French bread, ½ inch thick

2 teaspoons brandy or water

2 tablespoons chopped pecans

In medium skillet, melt butter over medium heat; add apples, sugar, and cinnamon. Sauté apples until tender; keep warm. In medium bowl, beat eggs, half-and-half, and vanilla; pour into shallow bowl. Heat griddle or skillet over medium heat and grease if necessary. Dip bread slices in egg mixture until thoroughly coated. Cook bread on hot griddle until golden brown on both sides. Add brandy and pecans to apples; cook over medium-high heat 30 seconds. Slice bread diagonally; top with apples and pecans. Serve with warm maple syrup if desired.

Three servings

Breakfast
Egg Dishes

Italian
Morning
Eggs

DUNBAR HOUSE, 1880

Murphys, California

1 cup sun-dried tomatoes (not
oil-packed)

2 tablespoons olive oil

3 cloves garlic, minced

½ cup water (or half water
and half wine)

4 eggs

¼ cup grated Parmesan cheese

1 tablespoon chopped fresh basil

1 package (10 ounces) frozen
chopped spinach

Thirty minutes before serving, in medium skillet, combine sun-dried tomatoes, olive oil, garlic, and water; let sit for 15 minutes. Sauté tomatoes over medium heat, 10 minutes or until soft and plump. Crack eggs on top of tomatoes. Sprinkle with Parmesan cheese and basil. Cover and cook about 5 minutes or until eggs are cooked to desired doneness (add more water if necessary). Meanwhile, microwave spinach as directed on package; drain well and pat dry. Place ¼ cup cooked spinach on each plate. Top spinach with tomatoes and one egg. Garnish with fresh basil leaves if desired.

Four servings

Eggs
Madison

MADISON STREET INN
Santa Clara, California

2 cups shredded lettuce

2 large avocados

8 eggs

1 cup salsa

1½ cups shredded sharp
Cheddar cheese

½ cup sour cream

4 black olives, cut in half

4 flour tortillas

*P*lace ½ cup shredded lettuce on each plate. Cut avocados in half, peel and remove pit. Slice each half horizontally to make two flat slices; place on individual plates. Meanwhile, poach eggs and heat salsa. Place 2 poached eggs on top of avocado slices. Spoon warm salsa over eggs. Sprinkle with shredded cheese. Garnish with sour cream and olive halves. Heat tortillas on hot griddle, 10 seconds on each side. Fold tortillas into fourths. Serve tortillas with eggs.

Four servings

Chiles
Rellenos

2 cans (4 ounces each) whole green chiles, drained	3 eggs
	1 cup sour cream
1½ cups shredded Monterey jack cheese	Salsa

*P*reheat oven to 350°F. Arrange chiles in bottom of greased 9-inch-square glass baking dish. Sprinkle cheese over chiles. In medium bowl, beat eggs and sour cream; pour over chiles and cheese. Bake about 25 minutes or until custard is firm in center. Serve warm with salsa.

Four servings

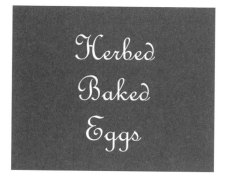

Herbed
Baked
Eggs

THE HANFORD HOUSE BED & BREAKFAST INN
Sutter Creek, California

4 large ham slices

6 eggs

1 teaspoon Dijon mustard

½ cup plain yogurt

1½ cups shredded Cheddar cheese, divided

2 teaspoons chopped fresh chives, divided

2 teaspoons chopped fresh parsley, divided

Preheat oven to 375°F. Place 1 slice ham in each greased large ramekin or custard cup. In medium bowl, beat eggs, mustard, and yogurt. Stir ½ cup of cheese, 1 teaspoon chives, and 1 teaspoon parsley into egg mixture; mix well. Spoon egg mixture evenly over ham in ramekins. Sprinkle remaining cheese and herbs over egg mixture. Bake 25 to 30 minutes or until golden and set. Garnish with sprigs of fresh herbs if desired.

Four servings

Creamy
Eggs with
Caviar

NORTH COAST COUNTRY INN
Gualala, California

2 tablespoons butter, divided

1 tablespoon all-purpose flour

½ cup sour cream

12 eggs

¼ teaspoon salt

Pinch white pepper

6 puff pastry rectangles, baked

Sour cream

Caviar

*I*n small saucepan, melt 1 tablespoon butter over medium heat. Stir in flour; cook until bubbly. Remove from heat and blend in sour cream. Return to heat and cook until bubbly and smooth; set aside. In large bowl, beat eggs, salt, and pepper. In large skillet, melt remaining tablespoon butter over medium heat. Pour in eggs and cook gently, lifting cooked portion to allow uncooked portion to flow underneath, until eggs are softly set. Remove from heat and gently stir in sour cream mixture. Serve eggs on baked puff pastry rectangles. Top with a dollop of sour cream and a sprinkling of caviar.

Six servings

Mock
Eggs
Benedict

6 slices Canadian bacon or turkey ham

6 slices (1 ounce each) Swiss cheese

12 eggs

¼ cup heavy (whipping) cream

Pepper to taste

Dash paprika

Grated Parmesan cheese

*P*reheat oven to 450°F. Spray 6 large ramekins or custard cups with nonstick cooking spray. Place one slice Canadian bacon in bottom of each dish; top with one slice Swiss cheese. Gently crack two eggs on top of cheese. Pour 1 teaspoon cream over each egg yolk. Bake 8 minutes or until egg whites are firm (yolks may be soft). Sprinkle with pepper, paprika, and Parmesan cheese. Serve with toasted English muffins if desired.

Six servings

Victorian
Eggs

HERITAGE PARK INN
San Diego, California

1 cup half-and-half	⅛ teaspoon pepper
2 eggs	⅛ teaspoon salt
⅓ cup all-purpose flour	4 green onions, finely diced
¼ teaspoon curry powder	½ cup sliced black olives
¼ teaspoon dried marjoram	¾ cup diced ham
¼ teaspoon dried basil	1 cup shredded Cheddar cheese
⅛ teaspoon garlic powder	½ cup diced tomato

In blender, combine half-and-half, eggs, flour, curry powder, marjoram, basil, garlic powder, pepper, and salt; blend until smooth. Spray 4 large ramekins or custard cups with nonstick cooking spray. Layer green onions, black olives, ham, and cheese in ramekins. Pour egg mixture into ramekins. Cover and refrigerate overnight. Remove from refrigerator. Preheat oven to 300°F. Uncover and bake 20 minutes. Sprinkle with diced tomato; bake 5 to 10 minutes longer or until set. Garnish with green onion if desired.

Four servings

Crab
Soufflé

FORBESTOWN BED & BREAKFAST INN
Lakeport, California

8 ounces imitation crab, chopped

1 cup shredded Cheddar cheese

1 cup shredded Monterey jack cheese

6 eggs

1 cup sour cream

1 tablespoon butter, melted

¼ cup all-purpose flour

½ teaspoon baking powder

¼ teaspoon salt

*P*reheat oven to 375°F. Spray 1½-quart soufflé dish with nonstick cooking spray. Layer crab and cheeses in bottom of dish. In blender, combine remaining ingredients; blend until smooth. Pour egg mixture over crab and cheeses in dish. Bake about 1 hour or until set.

Four servings

Mini
Cheese
Soufflés

THE PELENNOR BED & BREAKFAST
Mariposa, California

¼ cup butter	1 cup milk
¼ cup all-purpose flour	1 cup shredded Cheddar cheese
Dash paprika	4 eggs, separated
Dash cayenne pepper	

Preheat oven to 375°F. In medium saucepan, melt butter over medium heat. Stir in flour, paprika, and cayenne pepper. Whisk in milk and cook, stirring constantly, until smooth and slightly thickened. Add cheese and stir until melted; remove from heat. Beat egg yolks slightly; stir into cheese mixture. In separate bowl, beat egg whites until stiff; fold into cheese mixture. Spoon into 4 greased and floured large ramekins or custard cups. Bake 15 to 20 minutes or until puffed and golden brown. Serve immediately.

Four servings

Cornmeal
Soufflé

THE HEIRLOOM BED & BREAKFAST
Ione, California

3 tablespoons butter

2 tablespoons chopped green onions

¼ cup yellow cornmeal

½ teaspoon dried oregano

1¼ cups milk

¾ cup shredded Monterey jack cheese

4 eggs, separated

FRESH TOMATO SAUCE:

¼ cup butter or margarine

4 cups chopped fresh tomatoes

½ teaspoon dried basil

½ teaspoon salt

¼ teaspoon pepper

Preheat oven to 350°F. In medium saucepan, melt butter and sauté green onions. Stir in cornmeal and oregano. Add milk and cheese. Stir over medium heat until cheese is melted and sauce thickens; remove from heat. Stir in egg yolks. In separate bowl, beat egg whites until soft peaks form. Fold egg whites into cornmeal mixture. Pour into greased 1½-quart soufflé dish; set in pan of water. Bake 45 minutes or until puffed and golden. In medium saucepan, melt butter over medium heat. Add tomatoes and seasonings; simmer 30 minutes. Serve soufflé with warm tomato sauce (or canned crushed tomatoes if desired).

Four servings

Mayan
Maize
Tortilla Pie

THE GLENBOROUGH INN
Santa Barbara, California

2 flour tortillas (8 inches)

2 cans (15 ounces each) baby corn, drained, with 1 cup liquid reserved

1 tablespoon dried basil

2 cloves garlic, minced

1 can (4 ounces) chopped green chiles, drained

1 small onion, finely diced

1 can (14 ounces) pimientos, drained and diced

1 can (2 ounces) sliced black olives

⅓ cup shredded pepper jack cheese

4 eggs

1 teaspoon garlic powder

1 teaspoon ground cumin

1 teaspoon pepper

2 tablespoons lime juice

¼ cup nonfat dry milk powder

¼ cup all-purpose flour

*P*lace 1 tortilla on bottom of greased 9-inch pie plate. Top with layer of baby corn in circular fashion, with points toward middle. Sprinkle with basil, garlic, and green chiles. Layer with second tortilla and another layer of baby corn. Sprinkle with onion and pimientos. Top with black olives and cheese. In blender, combine eggs with remaining ingredients; blend 1 to 2 minutes. Pour egg mixture over layers. Cover and refrigerate at least 2 hours or overnight. Remove from refrigerator. Preheat oven to 350°F. Uncover and bake 45 to 60 minutes or until golden brown and set in middle. Cool 15 minutes before cutting. Serve with guacamole or salsa if desired.

Six servings

Italian
Zucchini
Frittata

2 tablespoons olive oil	6 eggs
1 small onion, chopped	1 teaspoon dried basil
1 clove garlic, minced	1 teaspoon dried oregano
1 medium zucchini, sliced	Salt and pepper, to taste
2 large Swiss chard leaves, chopped	1 cup grated Parmesan cheese

*P*reheat oven to 350°F. In medium skillet, sauté onion, garlic, zucchini, and Swiss chard in olive oil 5 to 8 minutes or until tender. Remove vegetables from heat; cool slightly. In large bowl, beat eggs with seasonings; stir in cheese. Spoon vegetables into greased 9-inch pie plate. Pour egg mixture over vegetables. Bake 25 to 30 minutes or until puffed and browned. Serve hot or cold.

Six servings

Hash
Brown
Quiche

LAVENDER HILL BED & BREAKFAST
Sonora, California

1 package (24 ounces) frozen shredded
hash brown potatoes (thawed)

⅓ cup butter, melted

¼ cup ricotta cheese

1 cup shredded Cheddar cheese

1 cup shredded Monterey jack cheese

1 cup diced ham

2 eggs

½ cup milk

⅛ teaspoon cayenne pepper

¼ teaspoon seasoning salt

Preheat oven to 425°F. Press hash brown potatoes into greased 9-inch quiche dish or pie plate. Brush with butter. Bake 25 minutes. Reduce oven temperature to 350°F. Spread potatoes with ricotta cheese, then sprinkle with cheeses and ham. In medium bowl, beat eggs, milk, cayenne pepper, and seasoning salt. Pour egg mixture over cheeses and ham. Bake 30 to 40 minutes or until set.

Six servings

Spinach
Mushroom
Quiche

TODD FARM HOUSE BED & BREAKFAST
Fort Bragg, California

1 (9-inch) pie shell, unbaked

½ teaspoon yellow mustard

2 teaspoons butter or margarine

½ cup chopped onion

½ cup sliced mushrooms

1 package frozen chopped spinach,
thawed and drained

1 cup shredded Swiss cheese

3 eggs

1 cup milk

½ teaspoon salt

Dash paprika

*P*reheat oven to 400°F. Bake pie shell according to package directions. Reduce oven temperature to 350°F. Spread mustard in
bottom of baked pie shell. In medium skillet, melt butter over
medium heat. Sauté onion, mushrooms, and spinach; spoon into pie shell.
Sprinkle with cheese. In large bowl, beat eggs, milk, and salt; pour over vegetables and cheese. Sprinkle with paprika. Bake 40 to 45 minutes or until
center is set.

Six servings

Vegetarian
Crustless
Quiche

FERRANDO'S HIDEAWAY
Point Reyes Station, California

3 to 4 tablespoons bread crumbs

1⅔ cups shredded Monterey jack
or Cheddar cheese

½ cup chopped onion

½ cup chopped shiitake mushrooms

1 can (14 ounces) artichoke hearts,
drained and chopped

3 eggs

⅔ cup milk

½ cup mayonnaise

1 tablespoon cornstarch

*P*reheat oven to 350°F. Spray 8-inch-square glass baking dish with nonstick cooking spray. Sprinkle dish generously with bread crumbs. Layer cheese, onion, mushrooms, and artichokes in baking dish. In large bowl, beat eggs, milk, mayonnaise, and cornstarch; pour over cheese and vegetables. Bake 35 to 45 minutes or until firm in center. Let sit 10 minutes before cutting.

Four servings

Ham and
Cheese
Breakfast Pie

1 can (4 ounces) chopped green chiles, drained	¾ cup diced ham
	4 eggs
¼ small Spanish onion, finely chopped	½ cup milk
1 small tomato, chopped	¼ teaspoon dried basil
½ cup shredded Monterey jack cheese	¼ teaspoon dried oregano
½ cup shredded Cheddar cheese	Salt and pepper, to taste

*P*reheat oven to 375°F. Spray 9-inch pie plate with nonstick cooking spray. Layer pie plate with chiles, onion, tomato, cheeses, and ham. In blender, combine eggs, milk, and seasonings; blend until smooth. Pour egg mixture into pie plate. Bake 30 to 35 minutes or until center is set.

Six servings

Green Chile
and
Potato Tart

THE STANFORD INN BY THE SEA
Mendocino, California

4 to 5 new red potatoes (unpeeled)

2 tablespoons olive oil

1 large onion, chopped

4 garlic cloves, minced

1 can (4 ounces) chopped green
chiles, drained

1 jar (7.25 ounces) roasted red bell
peppers, chopped

5 eggs

1 cup shredded Monterey jack cheese

1 cup shredded medium Cheddar cheese

Pinch crushed red pepper

¼ teaspoon salt

Dash pepper

Preheat oven to 375°F. Wash and boil potatoes until nearly cooked (potatoes should remain firm); set aside. When cool, cut into ¼-inch slices. In medium skillet, sauté onion and garlic in olive oil until soft; remove from heat. Add green chiles and roasted red peppers to onion mixture. In large bowl, beat eggs; stir in vegetables, cheeses, and seasonings. Layer potatoes in greased 10-inch deep-dish pie plate. Spoon half of egg mixture over potatoes. Repeat with second layer of potatoes and remaining egg mixture. Bake 30 to 35 minutes or until golden and set.

Six servings

Eggs for a Crowd

Bella
Torta

4 packages (10 ounces each) frozen
chopped spinach

16 eggs, divided

⅔ cup heavy (whipping) cream
or half-and-half

1 cup bread crumbs

⅓ cup pine nuts

½ teaspoon ground nutmeg

1 cup milk

1 teaspoon Italian seasonings

2 tablespoons butter

1½ cups chopped, rehydrated sun-dried
tomatoes (well drained if packed in
oil)

4 ounces thinly sliced Provolone cheese

½ teaspoon cracked black pepper

2 jars (6 ounces each) marinated
artichoke hearts, drained

*P*reheat oven to 350°F. Cook and completely drain all moisture from spinach. In medium bowl, mix spinach with 4 beaten eggs, cream, bread crumbs, pine nuts, and nutmeg; set aside. In large bowl, beat 12 eggs, milk, and Italian seasonings. In large skillet, melt butter and loosely scramble egg mixture (eggs should be moist). Spoon eggs evenly into greased 13-by-9-inch glass baking dish. Layer tomatoes evenly over scrambled eggs. Top with cheese, spinach mixture, and cracked pepper. Arrange artichoke hearts in rows on top of spinach mixture. Bake 40 minutes. Cool 5 minutes before cutting. *Note:* This dish can be prepared a day ahead.

Fifteen servings

Cheesy
Potato
Pie

6 eggs	½ teaspoon salt
½ cup milk	1 cup small curd cottage cheese
¼ cup butter, melted	4 cups shredded Colby-Monterey jack
2 tablespoons vegetable oil	or pepper jack cheese
½ cup all-purpose flour	12 ounces frozen shredded hash brown
1½ teaspoons baking powder	potatoes, thawed (plain or
Dash ground red pepper	Southwestern style)

Preheat oven to 350°F. In large bowl, beat eggs, milk, butter, and oil. Stir in flour, baking powder, ground red pepper, and salt. Add cheeses and slightly more than half of potatoes; mix well. Spray two 9-inch glass pie plates with nonstick cooking spray. Spread mixture evenly in bottom of pie plates. Top with remaining potatoes. Bake 35 minutes or until golden brown. Serve with salsa if desired.

Two pies (six servings each)

Eggs
for a
Gang

FAIRVIEW MANOR
Ben Lomond, California

12 eggs, beaten	*1 teaspoon Worcestershire sauce*
2 cans (15 ounces each) creamed corn	*4 cups shredded sharp Cheddar cheese*
1 can (7 ounces) chopped green	*1 teaspoon salt*
chiles, drained	*½ teaspoon pepper*

*P*reheat oven to 325°F. In large bowl, combine all ingredients and mix well. Pour into greased 13-by-9-inch glass baking dish. Bake 50 to 60 minutes or until set.

Ten servings

Sausage
Strata

THE GREY WHALE INN
Fort Bragg, California

1 package (12 ounces) breakfast
roll sausage

1 cup finely chopped onion

16 slices sourdough French bread, cut
into ½-inch cubes

2 cups shredded sharp Cheddar cheese

¼ cup margarine, melted

8 eggs

2½ cups milk

In large skillet, lightly brown sausage, breaking up into small pieces. Add onion; cook until golden. Drain off excess fat. In large bowl, toss bread cubes, cheese, margarine, and onion and sausage mixture. Spray 13-by-9-inch baking pan with nonstick cooking spray. Spread mixture evenly into pan. Beat eggs and milk together; pour over bread and sausage mixture. Cover with aluminum foil that has been sprayed with nonstick cooking spray. Refrigerate overnight. Remove from refrigerator 30 minutes before baking. Preheat oven to 350°F. Set pan in hot water bath (water should come up the sides of the casserole about ¾ inch). Bake covered 50 minutes. Uncover and bake 15 minutes longer or until golden. Cool 15 minutes before cutting.

Twelve servings

Artichoke
Mushroom
Strata

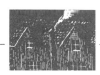

OLD MONTEREY INN
Monterey, California

8 eggs	1 cup shredded Swiss
2 cups milk	or Muenster cheese
2 tablespoons butter, melted	1 cup diced fresh mushrooms
10 slices white bread, crusts removed	2 tablespoon chopped fresh chives
and cut into ½-inch cubes	2 teaspoons dried tarragon
1 can (14 ounces) artichoke bottoms,	¼ teaspoon salt
drained and chopped	¼ teaspoon white pepper

*P*reheat oven to 375°F. In large bowl (or blender), beat eggs, milk, and butter. In large bowl, combine egg mixture with remaining ingredients; let sit 30 minutes. Pour mixture into 13-by-9-inch greased baking dish. Bake about 45 minutes or until puffy and golden. *Note:* This strata can also be baked in 8 large ramekins or custard cups for 30 minutes.

Eight servings

Sonoma County
Egg
Casserole

CAVANAGH INN
Petaluma, California

1 can (7 ounces) chopped green chiles

½ cup baking mix or all-purpose flour

4 cups shredded Monterey jack cheese

12 eggs

1 cup evaporated milk

1 cup cottage cheese

½ teaspoon baking powder

1 teaspoon salt

Pepper, to taste

Dash paprika

*P*reheat oven to 325°F. Spray 13-by-9-inch glass baking dish with nonstick cooking spray. In small bowl, toss chiles with baking mix; spread evenly into bottom of dish. Top with cheese. In large bowl, beat eggs, milk, cottage cheese, baking powder, salt, pepper, and paprika. Pour egg mixture over cheese. Bake 35 to 40 minutes or until light brown. Let rest 5 minutes before cutting. Serve with salsa, sour cream, and warm corn tortillas if desired.

Ten servings

Baked
Sour Cream
Omelet

STRAWBERRY CREEK INN
Idyllwild, California

½ loaf French bread, cut into ½-inch slices

1 cup shredded Gruyère cheese

1 cup shredded Monterey jack cheese

12 slices bacon, cooked and crumbled

4 green onions, chopped

8 eggs

1⅓ cups milk

⅓ cup white wine

1 teaspoon Dijon mustard

¼ teaspoon black pepper

⅛ teaspoon cayenne pepper

¾ cup sour cream

½ cup grated Parmesan cheese

Dash paprika

Preheat oven to 325°F. Spray 13-by-9-inch baking dish with non-stick cooking spray. Cover bottom of dish with bread slices. Sprinkle cheeses, bacon, and green onions over bread. In medium mixing bowl, beat eggs, milk, wine, mustard, black pepper, and cayenne pepper; pour over cheese and bread. Cover tightly with foil and bake 45 minutes or until set. Remove foil and spread with sour cream; sprinkle with Parmesan cheese and paprika. Bake uncovered about 10 minutes or until lightly browned. *Note:* This can be made the night before (let stand at room temperature 30 minutes before baking).

Twelve servings

Italian
Sausage
Frittata

LA CHAUMIÈRE, A COUNTRY INN . . . .
Calistoga, California

1½ pounds mild Italian bulk sausage	*3 large Swiss chard leaves, thinly sliced*
3 cups sliced fresh mushrooms	*1 cup shredded mild Cheddar cheese*
1 teaspoon garlic powder	*9 eggs*
2 tablespoons butter or margarine	*1¼ cups milk*
¼ cup white wine	*2 to 3 tablespoons Dijon mustard*

Preheat oven to 350°F. In large skillet, brown sausage; drain. Spread sausage evenly in greased 13-by-9-inch glass baking dish. Sauté mushrooms and garlic powder in butter and wine until almost all liquid is absorbed; spoon over sausage. Top with Swiss chard and cheese. In large bowl, beat eggs, milk, and Dijon mustard; pour evenly over all. Bake 1 hour or until middle is firm to the touch. Cover loosely with foil and let stand 15 minutes before cutting. Serve with sour cream, salsa, and chopped fresh chives if desired.

Eight servings

Artichoke Frittata

AMADOR HARVEST INN
Plymouth, California

1 cup thick and chunky salsa

1 can (14 ounces) artichoke hearts, drained and chopped

⅓ cup grated Parmesan cheese

1½ cups shredded Monterey jack cheese

1½ cups shredded sharp Cheddar cheese

6 eggs

1 cup sour cream

Preheat oven to 350°F. Spray 13-by-9-inch glass baking dish with nonstick cooking spray. Spread salsa evenly in bottom of dish; sprinkle with artichokes and cheeses. In medium bowl, beat eggs and sour cream. Pour egg mixture over artichokes and cheese. Bake 30 to 40 minutes or until set and slightly brown.

Eight servings

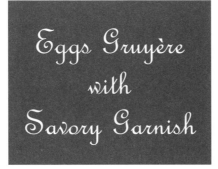

Eggs Gruyère
with
Savory Garnish

THE HEADLANDS INN
Mendocino, California

2 cups shredded Gruyère cheese

¼ cup butter, cut up

1 cup heavy (whipping) cream

1½ teaspoons dry mustard

½ teaspoon salt

⅛ teaspoon white pepper

12 eggs, lightly beaten

GARNISH:

2 medium tomatoes, cut into

½-inch slices

¼ cup butter

⅔ cup seasoned bread crumbs

⅓ cup unsalted sunflower nuts

*P*reheat oven to 325°F. Spray 13-by-9-inch glass baking dish with nonstick cooking spray. Spread cheese evenly in bottom of dish; dot with butter. Mix cream with seasonings; drizzle half of mixture over cheese. Slowly pour eggs over cheese; drizzle with remaining cream mixture. Bake about 35 minutes or until eggs are just set. During last 20 minutes of baking, place tomato slices on foil-lined baking sheet and set in oven on bottom shelf. In small saucepan, melt ¼ cup butter; stir in bread crumbs and sunflower nuts. After 10 minutes, remove tomatoes from oven and top with crumb mixture. Return to oven until eggs are set. Top each serving with tomato slice and garnish with parsley sprig if desired.

Eight servings

Hash
Brown
Casserole

THE SHORE HOUSE AT LAKE TAHOE
Tahoe Vista, California

1 package (24 ounces) frozen shredded hash brown potatoes, thawed

¼ cup butter, melted

10 slices bacon, cooked crisp

⅓ cup chopped, rehydrated sun-dried tomatoes

¼ cup chopped fresh parsley

2 cups shredded Cheddar cheese

8 eggs

1½ cups milk

½ teaspoon pepper

1 can (15 ounces) crushed tomato sauce

Preheat oven to 450°F. Press potatoes along bottom and sides of greased 13-by-9-inch baking pan. Brush potatoes with butter. Bake 25 minutes. Remove from oven. Reduce oven temperature to 350°F. Crumble bacon over potatoes. Sprinkle tomatoes, parsley, and cheese over bacon. In large mixing bowl, beat eggs, milk, and pepper. Pour egg mixture over cheese. Bake 45 minutes or until eggs are set. Let rest 10 minutes before cutting. Serve with crushed tomato sauce.

Eight servings

Fruit, Sides
& Sauces

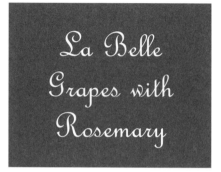

La Belle
Grapes with
Rosemary

BELLE EPOQUE BED & BREAKFAST INN
Napa, California

1 cup sugar	3 small melons
1 cup white wine	1 pound red seedless grapes
¼ cup water	1 pound green seedless grapes
1 sprig fresh rosemary	½ cup sour cream

Heat sugar, wine, water, and rosemary over medium heat 10 minutes. Cover and refrigerate overnight. Next day, cut melons in half and remove seeds. Carve melon with zigzag edges. Toss grapes with sugar syrup; spoon into melon halves. Top grapes with sour cream. Garnish with rosemary sprigs if desired.

Six servings

Baked
Banana
Crumble

ELK COVE INN
Elk, California

4 ripe firm bananas, peeled
¾ cup orange juice
1 teaspoon vanilla extract
½ cup all-purpose flour
½ cup quick-cooking oats

¾ cup brown sugar
½ teaspoon ground nutmeg
½ teaspoon salt
6 tablespoons cold butter

*P*reheat oven to 375°F. Slice bananas lengthwise and place, cut-sides up, in 4 greased oval ramekins or custard cups. In small bowl, combine orange juice and vanilla; drizzle over bananas. In large bowl, combine flour, oats, brown sugar, nutmeg, and salt. Cut in butter until mixture resembles small peas. Spoon crumble mixture evenly over fruit. Bake 15 to 20 minutes. Serve warm with vanilla ice cream if desired.

Four servings

Broiled
Blackberries

TIFFANY HOUSE BED & BREAKFAST
Redding, California

3 cups fresh blackberries   1 teaspoon vanilla extract

1 cup sour cream   1 cup brown sugar

*P*reheat oven to broil. Divide blackberries evenly among 6 small ramekins or custard cups. In small bowl, mix sour cream and vanilla; spoon over berries. Sprinkle with brown sugar (removing any lumps). Broil 1 minute or until sugar caramelizes (watch very carefully). Cover and refrigerate several hours or overnight. *Note:* This recipe can also be made with blueberries or sliced strawberries.

Six servings

Peaches
and
Cream

A WEAVER'S INN
Eureka, California

2 cups fresh sliced peaches

2 teaspoons almond-flavored liqueur

½ cup heavy (whipping) cream

1 egg yolk

¼ cup powdered sugar

½ teaspoon vanilla extract

Preheat oven to 400°F. Divide peaches evenly in 4 small ramekins or custard cups. Sprinkle with liqueur. Place ramekins on baking sheet. Whip cream to soft mounds; add egg yolk, powdered sugar, and vanilla and continue beating 1 minute. Spoon mixture evenly over peaches. Bake 3 minutes. Place under broiler about 1 minute (watch carefully) or until light golden brown. Serve immediately. *Note:* This recipe can also be made with fresh strawberries or raspberries and berry liqueur.

Four servings

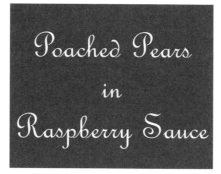

Poached Pears
in
Raspberry Sauce

ABIGAIL'S "ELEGANT VICTORIAN MANSION" BED & BREAKFAST

Eureka, California

4 Bosc pears, peeled

¼ cup maple syrup

Cinnamon sugar (1 tablespoon
granulated sugar mixed with ¼
teaspoon ground cinnamon)

4 teaspoons brown sugar

SAUCE:

3 cups fresh or frozen (thawed)
    raspberries

Granulated sugar

Cut thin slice off bottom so pears will stand up straight. Place pears upright in microwave dish. Spoon 1 tablespoon maple syrup over each pear. Sprinkle pears with cinnamon sugar mixture and brown sugar. Cover dish completely with plastic wrap; microwave on high 10 to 12 minutes or until pears are tender but not too soft. Meanwhile, place berries in blender; blend until smooth. Strain sauce through sieve. Add sugar to taste. Place sauce in medium saucepan and heat until warm. Place each poached pear on serving plate and cover with sauce, or spoon sauce on plate and set pear in center. Garnish with whole fresh berries if desired.

Four servings

Morning
Baked
Apples

GLENDEVEN INN & GALLERY
Little River, California

4 large tart apples, unpeeled

¼ cup brown sugar

1 teaspoon ground cinnamon

2 tablespoons currants

Zest of ½ orange

4 teaspoons butter, cut up

¾ cup apple juice

*P*reheat oven to 375°F. Wash apples and remove core, leaving ½ inch at bottom. Mix brown sugar, cinnamon, currants, and orange zest. Fill centers with sugar mixture and dot with butter. Place apples in 8-inch-square baking pan. Pour apple juice in pan. Bake 30 to 40 minutes, basting occasionally with juice, until apples are tender but not mushy. Serve with whipped cream if desired.

Four servings

Warm
Berry
Sauce

HOPE-MERRILL HOUSE
Geyserville, California

---

2 cups fresh or frozen raspberries

2 cups fresh or frozen strawberries

⅓ cup granulated sugar

⅓ cup freshly squeezed orange juice

3 tablespoons lemon juice

In medium saucepan, heat berries, sugar, orange juice, and lemon juice over medium heat. Cook, stirring constantly, until fruit begins to break up, about 5 minutes. Purée in food processor or blender. Return sauce to saucepan; heat until warm. Serve with bread pudding, waffles, or pancakes.

Two cups

Gala
Orange
Sauce

BUTTERFIELD BED & BREAKFAST
Julian, California

1 cup butter   ⅔ cup frozen orange juice concentrate
1 cup granulated sugar

In medium saucepan, melt butter over medium heat. Add sugar and orange juice concentrate; stir until sugar is dissolved. Remove from heat and cool slightly. Whip with whisk until thick and shiny. Serve warm over French toast, waffles, or bread pudding.

Two cups

Lemon
Curd

SIMPSON HOUSE INN
Santa Barbara, California

4 egg yolks plus 1 egg white   *¾ cup granulated sugar*

¼ cup butter   *Juice and grated rind of 1 lemon*

In medium bowl, beat egg yolks and egg white. In double boiler, melt butter. Stir in sugar, lemon juice, and lemon rind. Add eggs; mix well. Cook slowly over medium-low heat, stirring constantly, 15 minutes or until thickened. Cool before covering. Refrigerate up to 2 weeks.

One cup

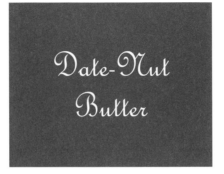

Date-Nut
Butter

HARKEY HOUSE BED & BREAKFAST
Yuba City, California

½ cup butter, softened   1 tablespoon granulated sugar

¼ cup finely chopped pitted dates   ¼ teaspoon vanilla extract

3 tablespoons chopped walnuts, toasted

In medium bowl, beat butter until smooth. Stir in remaining ingredients; mix well. Cover and refrigerate if not using immediately. Let butter stand at room temperature to soften before serving.

Three-fourths cup

Maricela's
Salsa

MADRONA MANOR
Healdsburg, California

3 ripe medium tomatoes, chopped   ½ cup finely chopped cilantro

½ cup finely chopped onion   2 teaspoons fresh lime juice

4 to 6 serrano chiles, finely chopped

In medium nonreactive (nonmetal) bowl, combine all ingredients; stir well. Excellent served with eggs.

Three cups

Basil Tomatoes
with
Pine Nuts

THE WEDGEWOOD INN

Jackson, California

---

2 large tomatoes, thinly sliced

2 tablespoons olive oil

or clarified butter

Garlic powder

2 tablespoons chopped fresh basil

Toasted pine nuts

*D*rizzle tomato slices with olive oil. Sprinkle with garlic powder, basil, and pine nuts. Top with broccoli flowerets, asparagus spears, or zucchini slices if desired. Nice accompaniment to egg dishes.

Six servings

Baked
Breakfast
Polenta

GINGERBREAD MANSION INN
Ferndale, California

---

4 cups chicken broth

1 cup polenta (coarse cornmeal)

4 tablespoons butter

½ cup shredded Cheddar

or Swiss cheese

3 tablespoons melted butter

¼ cup grated Parmesan cheese

*I*n large saucepan, bring chicken broth to boil over high heat. Whisk in polenta. Reduce heat and simmer about 20 minutes, stirring frequently, until polenta becomes thick and pulls away from sides of pan. Add 4 tablespoons butter and Cheddar cheese; stir until melted. Pour mixture into greased 9-by-5-inch loaf pan. When cool, cover and refrigerate several hours or overnight. Remove from refrigerator. Preheat oven to 350°F. Remove polenta from pan and cut into ¾-inch-thick slices. Cut slices in half diagonally and arrange in overlapping fashion in greased shallow casserole dish. Drizzle with 3 tablespoons melted butter. Sprinkle with Parmesan cheese. Bake 30 minutes or until golden brown. Serve warm.

Twelve servings

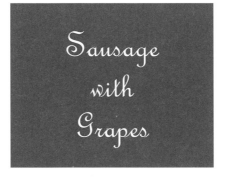

Sausage
with
Grapes

CAMELLIA INN
Healdsburg, California

6 fresh sweet Italian sausages   2 cups seedless green grapes
(about 1½ pounds)

Cut sausages into thirds. In large covered skillet, cook sausages in 1 cup water for 10 minutes. Add grapes. Cover and simmer 10 minutes. Uncover and cook over high heat until liquid begins to evaporate. Reduce heat and simmer uncovered 15 to 20 minutes; drain. Serve with polenta if desired.

Six servings

German
Potato
Pancakes

KRISTALBERG BED & BREAKFAST
Lucerne, California

2 medium boiling potatoes

2 eggs, slightly beaten

2 tablespoons all-purpose flour

½ teaspoon salt

2 green onions, finely chopped

1 clove garlic, minced

1 tablespoon butter

Peel and grate potatoes into large bowl. Stir in eggs, flour, salt, green onions, and garlic. In 12-inch skillet, melt butter over medium heat. Divide batter into four patties and place in skillet. Cook patties about 15 minutes over medium-low heat or until bottoms are golden brown. Turn and cook 10 to 12 minutes longer or until golden brown. Serve with sour cream and applesauce if desired.

Four pancakes

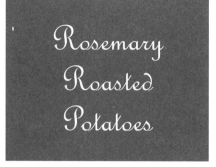

Rosemary
Roasted
Potatoes

THE JULIAN WHITE HOUSE BED & BREAKFAST

Julian, California

*4 medium potatoes, cut into
½-inch cubes

2 tablespoons olive oil

1 teaspoon dried sage*

*1 sprig fresh rosemary or 1 teaspoon
crushed dried rosemary leaves

Zest of 1 orange

½ teaspoon pepper*

Preheat oven to 375°F. Toss all ingredients in ungreased 13-by-9-inch baking pan. Bake on center rack 45 minutes, stirring occasionally, until potatoes are tender.

Four servings

Ballard
Home-Fried
Potatoes

THE BALLARD INN
Ballard, California

3 cups diced baby red potatoes

2 tablespoons olive oil or clarified butter

1 cup diced red bell pepper

2 to 3 green onions, chopped

Dash seasoning salt

In medium saucepan, cover potatoes with water and bring to boil. Reduce heat; cover and simmer 4 to 5 minutes. Strain potatoes in colander. In large skillet, heat olive oil. Add potatoes and cook 2 minutes without stirring. Add bell pepper and green onions; sauté until vegetables are tender and potatoes are evenly browned. Sprinkle with seasoning salt.

Four servings

Bed & Breakfast Inns

ABIGAIL'S BED & BREAKFAST
2120 G Street
Sacramento, CA 95816
(916) 441-5007 (800) 858-1568

ABIGAIL'S "ELEGANT VICTORIAN MANSION" BED & BREAKFAST LODGING ACCOMODATIONS
1406 "C" Street
Eureka, CA 95501
(707) 444-3144
fax (707) 442-5594
www.bnbcity.com/inns/20016

ADOBE INN
1473 Monterey Street
San Luis Obispo, CA 93401
(805) 549-0321
fax (805) 549-0383
jtowles@aol.com

AGATE COVE INN BED & BREAKFAST
11201 N. Lansing Street
PO Box 1150
Mendocino, CA 95460
(707) 937-0551; (800) 527-3111
fax (707) 937-0550
agate@mcn.org
www.agatecove.com

ALBION RIVER INN
PO Box 100
Albion, CA 95410
(707) 937-1919; (800) 479-7944
ari@mcn.org

AMADOR HARVEST INN
12455 Steiner Road
Plymouth, CA 95669
(209) 245-5512; (800) 217-2304

ANDERSON CREEK INN
12050 Anderson Valley Way
PO Box 217
Boonville, CA 95415
(707) 895-3091; (800) 552-6202

APPLE LANE INN
6265 Soquel Drive
Aptos, CA 95003
(408) 475-6868; (800) 649-8988
fax (408) 464-5790

APPLEWOOD INN
13555 Highway 116
Guerneville, CA 95446
(707) 869-9093
www.applewoodinn.com

ARBOR HOUSE INN
150 Clear Lake Avenue
Lakeport, CA 95453
(707) 263-6444

THE BALLARD INN
2436 Baseline Avenue
Ballard, CA 93463
(805) 688-7770; (800) 638-2466

BARRETTA GARDENS BED & BREAKFAST INN
700 S. Barretta Street
Sonora, CA 95370
(209) 532-6039
fax (209) 532-8257

BAYVIEW HOTEL, A COUNTRY INN
8041 Soquel Drive
Aptos, CA 95003
(408) 688-8654

BEARS AT THE BEACH BED & BREAKFAST
1047 Grand Avenue
San Diego, CA 92109-4118
(619) 272-2578

BEAZLEY HOUSE
1910 First Street
Napa, CA 94559
(707) 257-1649; (800) 559-1649
fax (707) 257-1518
jbeazley@napanet.net
www.napavalley.com/beazley/

BELLE EPOQUE
BED & BREAKFAST INN
1386 Calistoga Avenue
Napa, CA 94559
(707) 257-2161; (800) 238-8070
fax (707) 226-6314

BEN MADDOX HOUSE
601 N. Encina Street
Visalia, CA 93291
(209) 739-0721; (800) 401-9800
fax (209) 625-0420
muro@lightspeed.net

BLUE SPRUCE INN
2815 Main Street
Soquel, CA 95073
(408) 464-1137
pobrien@bluespruce.com
www.bluespruce.com

BOULDER CREEK
BED & BREAKFAST
4572 Ben Hur Road
Yosemite/Mariposa, CA 95338
(209) 742-7729; (800) 768-4752
fax (209) 742-5885
bcreekbb@yosemite.net
www.yosemite.net/mariposa/mhotels/
bouldercreek/

BUTTERFIELD
BED & BREAKFAST
2284 Sunset Drive
Box 1115
Julian, CA 92036
(760) 765-2179; (800) 379-4262

CAMELLIA INN
211 North Street
Healdsburg, CA 95448
(707) 433-8182; (800) 727-8182
fax (707) 433-8130
info@camelliainn.com
www.camelliainn.com

CAMPBELL RANCH INN
1475 Canyon Road
Geyserville, CA 95441
(707) 857-3476; (800) 959-3878
fax (707) 857-3239
www.campbellranchinn.com

CAPTAIN'S COVE INN
PO Box 803
Mendocino, CA 95460
(800) 780-7905
www.mcn.org

THE CARRIAGE HOUSE
1322 Catalina Street
Laguna Beach, CA 92651
(714) 494-8945

CARRIAGE HOUSE
BED & BREAKFAST
325 Mesa Road
PO Box 1239
Point Reyes, CA 94956
(415) 663-8627
www.carriagehousebb.com

CAVANAGH INN
10 Keller Street
Petaluma, CA 94952
(707) 765-4657; (888) 765-4658
fax (707) 769-0466

CHALFANT HOUSE
BED & BREAKFAST
213 Academy Street
Bishop, CA 93514
(760) 872-1790
www.touristguide.com/b&b/ca/chalfant

CHANNEL ROAD INN
219 W. Channel Road
Santa Monica, CA 90402
(310) 459-1920
fax (310) 454-9920
channelinn@aol.com
www.innaccess.com/cha

THE CHICHESTER-MCKEE
HOUSE
800 Spring Street
Placerville, CA 95667
(916) 626-1882 (800) 831-4008
inn@innercite.com
www.el-dorado.ca.us/~inn

CINNAMON BEAR
BED & BREAKFAST
1407 Kearney Street
St. Helena, CA 94574
(707) 963-4653

COAST GUARD HOUSE
HISTORIC INN
PO Box 117
Point Arena, CA 95468
(707) 882-2442; (800) 524-9320
fax (707) 882-3233
coast@mcn.org
www.coastguardhouse.com

COLUMBIA CITY HOTEL
Main Street, Columbia State Historic Park
PO Box 1870
Columbia, CA 95310
(209) 532-1479; (800) 532-1479
info@cityhotel.com
www.cityhotel.com

THE DALY INN
1125 H Street
Eureka, CA 95501
(707) 445-3638; (800) 321-9656
www.humboldt1.com/~dalyinn

DUNBAR HOUSE, 1880
PO Box 1375
Murphys, CA 95247
(209) 728-2897; (800) 692-6006
dunbarhs@goldrush.com
www.dunbarhouse.com

EAST BROTHER
LIGHT STATION
117 Park Place
Point Richmond, CA 94801
(510) 233-2385
www.bcg.net/brother/

ELK COVE INN
6300 S. Highway One
PO Box 367
Elk, CA 95432
(707) 877-3321; (800) 275-2967
www.elkcoveinn.com

EMMA NEVADA HOUSE
528 E. Broad Street
Nevada City, CA 95959
(916) 265-4415; (800) 916-EMMA
fax (916) 265-4416
emmanev@oro.net
www.riese.com/emma.htm

FAIRVIEW MANOR
245 Fairview Avenue
Ben Lomond, CA 95005
(408) 336-3355; (800) 553-8840

FERRANDO'S HIDEAWAY
PO Box 688
Point Reyes Station, CA 94956
(415) 663-1966; (800) 337-2636
fax (415) 663-1825
ferrando@nbn.com
www.ferrando.com

FLUME'S END
317 South Pine Street
Nevada City, CA 95959
(916) 265-9665; (800) 991-8118

FOOTHILL HOUSE
BED & BREAKFAST
3037 Foothill Boulevard
Calistoga, CA 94515
(707) 942-6933; (800) 942-6933
fax (707) 942-5692

FORBESTOWN
BED & BREAKFAST INN
825 N. Forbes Street
Lakeport, CA 95453
(707) 263-7858

FOUR SISTERS INNS
PO Box 3073
Monterey, CA 93942
(408) 649-0908; (800) 234-1425

THE GABLES
BED & BREAKFAST INN
4257 Petaluma Hill Road
Santa Rosa, CA 95404
(707) 585-7777; (800) GABLESN
innkeeper@thegablesinn.com
www.thegablesinn.com

THE GEORGE
ALEXANDER HOUSE
423 Matheson Street
Healdsburg, CA 95448
(707) 433-1358 (800) 310-1358
fax (707) 433-1367

GINGERBREAD MANSION INN
400 Berding Street
Ferndale, CA 95536
(707) 786-4000; (800) 952-4136
kenn@humboldt1.com
www.gingerbread-mansion.com

THE GLENBOROUGH INN
1327 Bath Street
Santa Barbara, CA 93101
(805) 966-0589; (888) 966-0589
fax (805) 564-8610
glenboro@silcom.com
www.silcom.com/~glenboro

GLENDEVEN
INN & GALLERY
8221 North Highway One
Little River, CA 95456
(707) 937-0083; (800) 822-4536
fax (707) 937-6108
www.innaccess.com/gdi/

GLENELLY INN
5131 Warm Springs Road
Glen Ellen, CA 95442
(707) 996-6720
fax (707) 996-5227
www.vom.com/glenelly/

THE GRAVENSTEIN INN
3160 Hicks Road
Sebastopol, CA 95472-2413
(707) 829-0493
gravensteininn@metro.net
www.metro.net/gravensteininn/

THE GREY WHALE INN
615 North Main Street
Fort Bragg, CA 95437
(707) 964-0640; (800) 382-7244
gwhale@mcn.org
www.innaccess.com/gwi

HAMMONS HOUSE INN
BED & BREAKFAST
22963 Robertson Ranch Road
Sonora, CA 95370
(209) 532-7921
fax (209) 586-4935
hammons@hammonshouseinn.com
www.hammonshouseinn.com

THE HANFORD HOUSE
BED & BREAKFAST INN
61 Hanford Street
PO Box 1450
Sutter Creek, CA 95685
(209) 267-0747; (800) 871-5839
fax (209) 267-1825
bobcat@hanfordhouse.com
www.hanfordhouse.com

HARKEY HOUSE
BED & BREAKFAST
212 C Street
Yuba City, CA 95991
(916) 674-1942

HARTLEY HOUSE
BED & BREAKFAST INN
700 22nd Street
Sacramento, CA 95816-4012
(916) 447-7829; (800) 831-5806
fax (916) 447-1820
randy@hartleyhouse.com
www.hartleyhouse.com

THE HEADLANDS INN
Corner of Howard and Albion Streets
PO Box 132
Mendocino, CA 95460
(707) 937-4431
fax (707) 937-0421
www.headlandsinn.com

THE HEIRLOOM
BED & BREAKFAST
214 Shakeley Lane
PO Box 322
Ione, CA 95640
(209) 274-4468; (888) 628-7896

HERITAGE PARK INN
2470 Heritage Park Row
San Diego, CA 92110
(619) 299-6832; (800) 995-2470
fax (619) 299-9465
innkeeper@heritageparkinn.com
www.heritageparkinn.com

HOMESTEAD
BED & BREAKFAST
4924 Highway 79
PO Box 1208
Julian, CA 92036
(760) 765-1536
fax (760) 765-1578

THE HONOR MANSION
14891 Grove Street
Healdsburg, CA 95448
(707) 433-4277; (800) 554-4667
fax (707) 431-7173
www.honormansion.com

HOPE-MERRILL HOUSE
21253 Geyserville Avenue
PO Box 42
Geyserville, CA 95441
(707) 857-3356

THE INK HOUSE
BED & BREAKFAST
1575 St. Helena Highway at
Whitehall Lane
St. Helena, CA 94574
(707) 963-3890
inkhousebb@aol.com
www.napavalley.com/inkhouse/

THE INN AT OCCIDENTAL
3657 Church Street
PO Box 857
Occidental, CA 95465
(707) 874-1047; (800) 522-6324
innkeeper@innatoccidental.com
www.innatoccidental.com

INN AT PLAYA DEL REY
435 Culver Boulevard
Playa del Rey, CA 90293
(310) 574-1920
fax (310) 574-9920
playainn@aol.com
www.innaccess.com/pdr

INN ON SUMMER HILL
2520 Lillie Avenue
Summerland, CA 93067
(805) 969-9998
info@innonsummerhill.com
www.innonsummerhill.com

INN ON TOMALES BAY
22555 Highway One
Marshall, CA 94940
(415) 663-9002
www.ptreyeslight.com

THE INN SAN FRANCISCO
943 South Van Ness Avenue
San Francisco, CA 94110
(415) 641-0188; (800) 359-0913
fax (415) 641-1701

JOSHUA GRINDLE INN
44800 Little Lake Road
PO Box 647
Mendocino, CA 95460
(707) 937-4143; (800) GRINDLE
info@joshgrin.com
www.joshgrin.com

JOSHUA TREE INN
BED & BREAKFAST
61259 29 Palms Highway
PO Box 340
Joshua Tree, CA 92252
(619) 366-1188; (800) 366-1444
fax (619) 366-3805

J. PATRICK HOUSE
BED & BREAKFAST
2990 Burton Drive
Cambria, CA 93428
(805) 927-3812; (800) 341-5258
jph@jpatrickhouse.com
www.jpatrickhouse.com

THE JULIAN WHITE HOUSE
BED & BREAKFAST
PO Box 824
Julian, CA 92036
(760) 765-1764; (800) WHTHOUS
stay@julian-whitehouse-bnb.com

KRISTALBERG
BED & BREAKFAST
½ mile off Highway 20 at Bruner Drive
PO Box 1629
Lucerne, CA 95458
(707) 274-8009
kristalberg@webtv.net

LA CHAUMIÈRE,
A COUNTRY INN . . . .
1301 Cedar Street
Calistoga, CA 94515
(707) 942-5139; (800) 474-6800
fax (707) 942-5199

LAVENDER HILL
BED & BREAKFAST
683 S. Barretta
Sonora, CA 95370
(209) 532-9024; (800) 446-1333 x290
lavender@sonnet.com
www.sonnet.com/dancers/bandb/
lavender/

LOMA VISTA
BED & BREAKFAST
33350 La Serena Way
Temecula, California 92591
(909) 676-7047
fax (909) 676-0077

LOST WHALE INN
3452 Patrick's Point
Trinidad, CA 95570
(707) 677-3425; (800) 677-7859

MADISON STREET INN
1390 Madison Street
Santa Clara, CA 95050
(408) 249-5541; (800) 491-5541
fax (408) 249-6676
madstinn@aol.com

MADRONA MANOR
1001 Westside Road
Healdsburg, CA 95448
(707) 433-4231; (800) 258-4003
fax (707) 433-0703
madronaman@aol.com
www.madronamanor.com/htmlpages/
madrona/index.html

MAYFIELD HOUSE
BED & BREAKFAST
236 Grove Street
PO Box 5999
Tahoe City, CA 96145
(916) 583-1001

McCLOUD RIVER INN
325 Lawndale Court
McCloud, CA 96057
(916) 964-2130; (800) 261-7831
mort@snowcrest.net
www.riverinn.com

MEADOW CREEK RANCH
BED & BREAKFAST
2669 Triangle Road
Mariposa, CA 95338
(209) 966-3843

MELITTA STATION INN
5850 Melita Road
Santa Rosa, CA 95409
(707) 538-7712; (800) 504-3099

MENDOCINO VILLAGE INN
44860 Main Street
PO Box 626
Mendocino, CA 95460
(707) 937-0246; (800) 882-7029
mendoinn@aol.com
www.mendocinoinn.com

MESA VERDE PLANTATION
BED & BREAKFAST
33038 Sierra Highway 198
Lemon Cove, California 93244
(209) 597-2555; (800) 240-1466
fax (209) 597-2551
mvpbb@psnw.com
www.psnw.com/~mvpbb

MURPHY'S INN
318 Neal Street
Grass Valley, CA 95945
(916) 273-6873; (800) 895-2488

NORTH COAST
COUNTRY INN
34591 S. Highway One
Gualala, CA 95445
(707) 884-4537; (800) 959-4537

OLD MONTEREY INN
500 Martin Street
Monterey, CA 93940
(408) 375-8284; (800) 350-2344
fax (408) 375-6730
omi@oldmontereyinn.com
www.innaccess.com/omi

OLD THYME INN
779 Main Street
Half Moon Bay, CA 94019
(415) 726-1616
fax (415) 726-6394
oldthyme@coastside.net
www.inntraveler.com/oldthyme/

ORCHARD HILL
COUNTRY INN
2502 Washington Street
PO Box 425
Julian, CA 92036-0425
(760) 765-1700; (800) 71-ORCHARD

THE PALM HOTEL
BED & BREAKFAST
10382 Willow Street
Jamestown, CA 95327
(209) 984-3429

THE PELENNOR
BED & BREAKFAST
3871 Highway 49 South
Mariposa, CA 95338
(209) 966-2832

PELICAN COVE INN
320 Walnut Avenue
Carlsbad, CA 92008
(760) 434-5995
(888) PELCOVE
www.pelican-cove.com/pelican

THE PHILO POTTERY INN
8550 Highway 128
PO Box 166
Philo, CA 95466
(707) 895-3069
www.innaccess.com/phi/

PILLAR POINT INN
380 Capistrano Road
Princeton, CA 94018
PO Box 388
El Granada, CA 94018
(415) 728-7377; (800) 400-8281
www.pillar-point.com

PRUFROCK'S GARDEN INN
600 Linden Avenue
Carpinteria, CA 93013
(805) 566-9696; (888) PRUFROK

RACHEL'S INN
PO Box 134
Mendocino, CA 95460
(707) 937-0088; (800) 347-9252
fax (707) 937-3620
www.rachelsinn.com

RANCHO SAN GREGORIO
Route 1, Box 54
San Gregorio, CA 94074
(415) 747-0810
fax (415) 747-0184
rsgleebud@aol.com
www.virtualcities.com/ons/ca/b/
cab8501.htm

ROCKWOOD GARDENS
BED & BREAKFAST
5155 Tip Top Road
Mariposa, CA 95338
(209) 742-6817; (800) 859-8862
fax (209) 742-7400

RYAN HOUSE, 1855
153 S. Shepherd Street
Sonora, CA 95370
(209) 533-3445 (800) 831-4897
www.ryanhouse.com

SCOTT COURTYARD
1443 2nd Street
Calistoga, CA 94515
(707) 942-0948; (800) 942-1515

SERENITY
BED & BREAKFAST INN
15305 Bear Cub Drive
Sonora, CA 95370
(209) 533-1441; (800) 426-1441
serenity@mlode.com
www.serenity-inn.com

THE SHORE HOUSE
AT LAKE TAHOE
7170 N. Lake Boulevard
PO Box 343
Tahoe Vista, CA 96148
(916) 546-7270; (800) 207-5160
fax (916) 546-7130
shorehse@inntahoe.com
www.inntahoe.com

SILVER ROSE INN & SPA
351 Rosedale Road
Calistoga, California 94515
(707) 942-9581; (800) 995-9381
www.silverrose.com

SIMPSON HOUSE INN
121 E. Arrellaga Street
Santa Barbara, CA 93101
(805) 963-7067; (800) 676-1280
simpsonhouse@compuserve.com
www.simpsonhouseinn.com

THE STANFORD INN
BY THE SEA
Coast Highway 1 and
Comptche-Ukiah Road
PO Box 487
Mendocino, CA 95460
(707) 937-5615; (800) 331-8884
fax (707) 937-0305

STRAWBERRY CREEK INN
PO Box 1818
Idyllwild, CA 92549
(909) 659-3202; (800) 262-8969

SUTTER CREEK INN
75 Main Street
Sutter Creek, CA 95685
(209) 267-5606
info@suttercreekinn.com
www.suttercreekinn.com

THE SWEDISH HOUSE
BED & BREAKFAST
10009 East River Street
Truckee, CA 96161
(916) 587-0400

TIFFANY HOUSE
BED & BREAKFAST
1510 Barbara Road
Redding, CA 96003
(916) 244-3225
tiffanyhse@aol.com
www.sylvia.com/tiffany.htm

TODD FARM HOUSE
BED & BREAKFAST
100 Highway 20
Fort Bragg, CA 95437
(707) 964-6575; (800) 722-1829

TRES PALMAS
BED & BREAKFAST
73135 Tumbleweed Lane
Palm Desert, CA 92260
(760) 773-9858 (800) 770-9858

VICHY HOT SPRINGS
RESORT & INN
2605 Vichy Springs Road
Ukiah, CA 95482
(707) 462-9515
fax (707) 462-9516
vichy@pacific.net

VINEYARD COUNTRY INN
201 Main Street
St. Helena, CA 94574
(707) 963-1000

A WEAVER'S INN
1440 B Street
Eureka, CA 95501
(707) 443-8119; (800) 992-8119
fax (707) 443-7923

weavrinn@humboldt1.com
www.humboldt1.com/~weavrinn

THE WEDGEWOOD INN
11941 Narcissus Road
Jackson, CA 95642
(209) 296-4300; (800) WEDGEWD
fax (209) 296-4301
vic@wedgewoodinn.com
www.wedgewoodinn.com

THE WHALE WATCH INN
35100 Highway One
Gualala, CA 95445
(707) 884-3667; (800) WHALE42
www.webering.com/whalepreview/
index.htm

WHITEGATE INN
BED & BREAKFAST
499 Howard Street
PO Box 150
Mendocino, CA 95460
(707) 937-4892; (800) 531-7282
staff@whitegateinn.com
www.whitegateinn.com

WHITE HORSE INN
BED & BREAKFAST
PO Box 2326
Mammoth Lakes, CA 93546
(760) 924-3656; (800) 982-5657
jct1@qnet.com

THE YOSEMITE PEREGRINE
BED & BREAKFAST
7509 Henness Circle
Yosemite, CA 95389
(209) 372-8517; (800) 396-3639
fax (209) 372-4241
kpitts@inreach.com
www.yosemitewest.com

THE ZABALLA HOUSE
BED & BREAKFAST
324 Main Street
Half Moon Bay, CA 94019
(415) 726-9123
fax (415) 726-3921
www.whistlere.com/zaballa

Index

A

Abigail's Bed & Breakfast, 17
Abigail's "Elegant Victorian Mansion"
  Bed & Breakfast, 231
Adobe Inn, 97
Agate Cove Inn Bed & Breakfast, 111
Albion River Inn, 137
Almonds
  Breakfast Muesli, 77
  Cranberry Buttermilk Scones, 7
  Fresh Rhubarb Cake, 71
  Homestead Granola, 81
  Raspberry Cream Cheese Coffee
    Cake, 53
  White Fruit Cake, 73
Amador Harvest Inn, 215
Anderson Creek Inn, 95
Apfel Pfannkuchen, 131
Apple Coffee Cake, 59
Apple-Cranberry Muffins, 25
Apple Lane Inn, 65
Apple Oatmeal Crisp, 83
Apple Oven-Baked Pancake, 133
Apple-Pecan French Toast, 159
Apple Pie Bread Pudding, 93
Apples
  Apfel Pfannkuchen, 131
  Apple Coffee Cake, 59
  Apple-Cranberry Muffins, 25
  Apple Oatmeal Crisp, 83
  Apple Oven-Baked Pancake, 133
  Apple-Pecan French Toast, 159
  Applesauce Cake, 67
  Apple Walnut Pancakes, 127
  Caramel Apple French Toast
  German Apple Pancakes, 123
  Morning Baked Apples, 233
Applesauce Cake, 67
Apple Walnut Pancakes, 127
Applewood Inn, 151
Apricot Cornmeal Muffins, 23

Apricots
  Apricot Cornmeal Muffins, 23
  Breakfast Muesli, 77
  White Fruit Cake, 73
Arbor House Inn, 159
Artichoke Frittata, 215
Artichoke-Mushroom Strata, 207
Artichokes
  Artichoke Frittata, 215
  Artichoke-Mushroom Strata, 207
  Bella Torta, 199
  Vegetarian Breakfast Quiche, 191

B

Bacon
  Baked Sour Cream Omelet, 211
  Mock Eggs Benedict, 173
  Sonoma County Egg Casserole, 219
Baked Banana Crumble, 225
Baked Breakfast Polenta, 247
Baked Sour Cream Omelet, 211
Ballard Home-Fried Potatoes, 255
The Ballard Inn, 255
Banana Nut Bread Pudding, 95
Bananas
  Baked Banana Crumble, 225
  Banana Nut Bread Pudding, 95
  Seasonal Fruit Crepes, 135
  Spiced Banana Cake, 61
Barretta Gardens Bed & Breakfast Inn,
  193
Basil Tomatoes with Pine Nuts, 245
Bayview Hotel, A Country Inn, 67
Bears at the Beach Bed & Breakfast, 143
Beazley House, 51
Bella Torta, 199
Belle Epoque Bed & Breakfast Inn, 223
Ben Maddox House, 155
Blackberries
  Broiled Blackberries, 227
  Cran-Blackberry Muffins, 31

Blintzes
    Cheese Blintz Soufflé, 107
    Cottage Cheese Blintz, 101
Blueberries
    Blueberry Cream Cheese Coffee Cake, 65
    Breakfast Berry Pudding, 91
    Fluffy Blueberry Pancakes, 121
Blueberry Cream Cheese Coffee Cake, 65
Blue Spruce Inn, 91
Boulder Creek Bed & Breakfast, 131
Breads
    Cinnamon Rolls, 109
    English Muffin Bread, 39
    Espresso Biscotti, 111
    Eye-Opener Jalapeño Corn Bread, 37
    Hawaiian Bread, 43
    Irish Soda Bread, 41
    Low-Fat Pineapple Bread, 51
    Pecan Pumpkin Bread, 45
    Strawberry Nut Bread, 47
    Tart Lemon Tea Bread, 49
    Walnut Shortbread, 113
    See also French toast, Muffins, Scones
Breakfast Berry Pudding, 91
Breakfast Muesli, 77
Broiled Blackberries, 227
Butterfield Bed & Breakfast, 237

C

Cakes
    Applesauce Cake, 67
    Chocolate Zucchini Rum Cake, 63
    Fresh Rhubarb Cake, 71
    Spiced Banana Cake, 61
    White Fruit Cake, 73
    See also Coffee cakes
Camellia Inn, 249
Campbell Ranch Inn, 53
Captain's Cove Inn, 25
Caramel Apple French Toast, 147
The Carriage House, 15
Carriage House Bed & Breakfast, 139

Casseroles
    Artichoke-Mushroom Strata, 207
    Baked Sour Cream Omelet, 211
    Bella Torta, 199
    Eggs for a Gang, 203
    Eggs Gruyère with Savory Garnish, 217
    Hash Brown Casserole, 219
    Sausage Strata, 205
    Sonoma County Egg Casserole, 209
    See also Frittatas
Cavanagh Inn, 209
Caviar
    Creamy Eggs with Caviar, 171
Chalfant House Bed & Breakfast, 109
Channel Road Inn, 61
Cheddar cheese
    Artichoke Frittata, 215
    Baked Breakfast Polenta, 247
    Crab Soufflé, 177
    Eggs for a Gang, 203
    Eggs Madison, 165
    Eye-Opener Jalapeño Corn Bread, 37
    Green Chile and Potato Tart, 195
    Ham and Cheese Breakfast Pie, 193
    Hash Brown Casserole, 219
    Hash Brown Quiche, 187
    Herbed Baked Eggs, 169
    Italian Sausage Frittata, 213
    Mini Cheese Soufflés, 179
    Sausage Strata, 205
    Vegetarian Breakfast Quiche, 191
    Victorian Eggs, 175
Cheese
    Artichoke Frittata, 215
    Artichoke-Mushroom Strata, 207
    Baked Breakfast Polenta, 247
    Baked Sour Cream Omelet, 211
    Bella Torta, 199
    Cheesy Potato Pie, 201
    Chiles Rellenos, 167
    Cornmeal Soufflé, 181
    Crab Soufflé, 177

Eggs for a Gang, 203
Eggs Gruyère with Savory Garnish, 217
Eggs Madison, 165
Eye-Opener Jalapeño Corn Bread, 37
Green Chile and Potato Tart, 195
Ham and Cheese Breakfast Pie, 193
Hash Brown Casserole, 219
Hash Brown Quiche, 187
Herbed Baked Eggs, 169
Italian Morning Eggs, 163
Italian Sausage Frittata, 213
Italian Zucchini Frittata, 185
Mini Cheese Soufflés, 179
Mock Eggs Benedict, 173
Sausage Strata, 205
Spinach Mushroom Quiche, 189
Vegetarian Breakfast Quiche, 191
Victorian Eggs, 175
See also specific cheese
Cheese Blintz Soufflé, 107
Cheesy Potato Pie, 201
Cherries
Breakfast Muesli, 77
Cherry Orange Scones, 9
Crunchy Nut Granola, 79
Espresso Biscotti, 111
Fresh Cherry Cobbler, 85
Cherry Orange Scones, 9
The Chichester-McKee House, 55
Chiles
Chiles Rellenos, 167
Eggs for a Gang, 203
Green Chile and Potato Tart, 195
Ham and Cheese Breakfast Pie, 193
Maricela's Salsa, 243
Mayan Maize Tortilla Pie, 183
Sonoma County Egg Casserole, 209
Chiles Rellenos, 167

Chocolate
Chocolate Zucchini Rum Cake, 63
Espresso Biscotti, 111
Mimosa Truffles, 115
Chocolate Zucchini Rum Cake, 63
Cinnamon Bear Bed & Breakfast, 5
Cinnamon-Glazed Scones, 5
Cinnamon Raisin Breakfast Custard, 99
Cinnamon Rolls, 109
Coast Guard House Historic Inn, 21
Cobblers
Apple Oatmeal Crisp, 83
Baked Banana Crumble, 225
Fresh Cherry Cobbler, 85
Coffee Cakes
Apple Coffee Cake, 59
Blueberry Cream Cheese Coffee Cake, 65
Plum Coffee Cake, 69
Pumpkin Cranberry Coffee Cake, 55
Raspberry Cream Cheese Coffee Cake, 53
Sour Cream Coffee Cake, 57
See also Cakes
Columbia City Hotel, 23
Corn
Eggs for a Gang, 203
Eye-Opener Jalapeño Corn Bread, 37
Mayan Maize Tortilla Pie, 183
Cornmeal
Apricot Cornmeal Muffins, 23
Baked Breakfast Polenta, 247
Cornmeal and Oat Waffles, 139
Cornmeal Soufflé, 181
Eye-Opener Jalapeño Corn Bread, 37
Cornmeal and Oat Waffles, 139
Cornmeal Soufflé, 181
Cottage cheese
Cheesy Potato Pie, 201
Cottage Cheese Blintz, 101
Sonoma County Egg Casserole, 209
Cottage Cheese Blintz, 101
Crab Soufflé, 177

Cranberries
  Apple-Cranberry Muffins, 25
  Breakfast Muesli, 77
  Cranberry Buttermilk Scones, 7
  Cran-Blackberry Muffins, 31
  Espresso Biscotti, 111
  Oatmeal and Cranberry Soufflé, 103
  Pumpkin Cranberry Coffee Cake, 55
Cranberry Buttermilk Scones, 7
Cran-Blackberry Muffins, 31
Cream cheese
  Apple Pie Bread Pudding, 93
  Blueberry Cream Cheese Coffee
    Cake, 65
  Breakfast Berry Pudding, 91
  Decadent French Toast Soufflé, 105
  Oatmeal and Cranberry Soufflé, 103
  Peach-Stuffed French Toast, 149
  Raspberry Cream Cheese Coffee
    Cake, 53
Creamy Eggs with Caviar, 171
Crepes
  Seasonal Fruit Crepes, 135
Crunchy Nut Granola, 79
Currants
  Morning Baked Apples, 233
  Oatmeal Buttermilk Pancakes, 119
Custard
  Cinnamon Raisin Breakfast Custard,
    99
  Fresh Fig Baked Custard, 97
  Rum Custard French Toast, 145
  See also Pudding

D-E
The Daly Inn, 31
Date-Nut Butter, 241
Date Pecan Scones, 11
Dates
  Date-Nut Butter, 241
  Date Pecan Scones, 11
  Pecan Pumpkin Bread, 45
  Pumpkin Pie Muffins, 27

Decadent French Toast Soufflé, 105
Dunbar House, 1880, 163
East Brother Light Station, 145
Egg dishes
  Artichoke Frittata, 215
  Artichoke-Mushroom Strata, 207
  Baked Sour Cream Omelet, 211
  Bella Torta, 199
  Cheesy Potato Pie, 201
  Chiles Rellenos, 167
  Cornmeal Soufflé, 181
  Crab Soufflé, 177
  Creamy Eggs with Caviar, 171
  Eggs for a Gang, 203
  Eggs Gruyère with Savory Garnish,
    217
  Eggs Madison, 165
  Green Chile and Potato Tart, 195
  Ham and Cheese Breakfast Pie, 193
  Hash Brown Casserole, 219
  Hash Brown Quiche, 187
  Herbed Baked Eggs, 169
  Italian Morning Eggs, 163
  Italian Sausage Frittata, 213
  Italian Zucchini Frittata, 185
  Mayan Maize Tortilla Pie, 183
  Mini Cheese Soufflés, 179
  Mock Eggs Benedict, 173
  Sausage Strata, 205
  Sonoma County Egg Casserole, 209
  Spinach Mushroom Quiche, 189
  Vegetarian Breakfast Quiche, 191
  Victorian Eggs, 175
Eggs for a Gang, 203
Eggs Gruyère with Savory Garnish, 217
Eggs Madison, 165
Elk Cove Inn, 225
Emma Nevada House, 141
English Muffin Bread, 39
Espresso Biscotti, 111
Eye-Opener Jalapeño Corn Bread, 37

F

Fairview Manor, 203
Ferrando's Hideaway, 191
Figs
    Fresh Fig Baked Custard, 97
Fluffy Blueberry Pancakes, 121
Flume's End, 167
Foothill House Bed & Breakfast, 105
Forbestown Bed & Breakfast Inn, 177
Four Sisters Inns, 57
French toast
    Apple-Pecan French Toast, 159
    Caramel Apple French Toast, 147
    Lemon-Poppy Seed French Toast, 153
    Peach-Stuffed French Toast, 149
    Pineapple French Toast, 155
    Portuguese French Toast, 157
    Rum Custard French Toast, 145
    Sunday's Baked French Toast, 151
Fresh Cherry Cobbler, 85
Fresh Fig Baked Custard, 97
Fresh Rhubarb Cake, 71
Frittatas
    Artichoke Frittata, 215
    Italian Sausage Frittata, 213
    Italian Zucchini Frittata, 185
    See also Casseroles, Quiches
Fruit dishes
    Baked Banana Crumble, 255
    Broiled Blackberries, 227
    La Belle Grapes with Rosemary, 223
    Morning Baked Apples, 233
    Peaches and Cream, 229
    Poached Pears In Raspberry
        Sauce, 231

G

The Gables Bed & Breakfast Inn, 125
Gala Orange Sauce, 237
The George Alexander House, 13
German Apple Pancakes, 123
German Potato Pancakes, 251
Gingerbread Mansion Inn, 247

Gingerbread Muffins, 15
Ginger-Pear Muffins, 21
The Glenborough Inn, 183
Glendeven Inn & Gallery, 233
Glenelly Inn, 89
Granola
    Breakfast Muesli, 77
    Crunchy Nut Granola, 79
    Homestead Granola, 81
Grapes
    La Belle Grapes with Rosemary, 223
    Sausage with Grapes, 249
The Gravenstein Inn, 127
Green Chile and Potato Tart, 195
The Grey Whale Inn, 205
Gruyère cheese
    Baked Sour Cream Omelet, 211
    Eggs Gruyère with Savory Garnish,
        217

H

Ham
    Ham and Cheese Breakfast Pie, 193
    Hash Brown Quiche, 187
    Herbed Baked Eggs, 169
    Victorian Eggs, 175
Ham and Cheese Breakfast Pie, 193
Hammons House Inn Bed & Breakfast,
    63
The Hanford House Bed & Breakfast
    Inn, 169
Harkey House Bed & Breakfast, 241
Hartley House Bed & Breakfast Inn, 11
Hash Brown Casserole, 219
Hash Brown Quiche, 187
Hawaiian Bread, 43
Hazelnuts
    Apple Walnut Pancakes, 127
    Cran-Blackberry Muffins, 31
    Hazelnut Waffles with Peaches, 137
Hazelnut Waffles with Peaches, 137
The Headlands Inn, 217
The Heirloom Bed & Breakfast, 181

Herbed Baked Eggs, 169
Heritage Park Inn, 175
Homestead Bed & Breakfast, 81
Homestead Granola, 81
Honey
    Crunchy Nut Granola, 79
    Homestead Granola, 81
    Whole Wheat Belgian Waffles, 143
The Honor Mansion, 9
Hope-Merrill House, 235

I - K

The Ink House Bed & Breakfast, 199
The Inn at Occidental, 129
Inn at Playa del Rey, 49
Inn on Summer Hill, 115
Inn on Tomales Bay, 135
The Inn San Francisco, 47
Irish Soda Bread, 41
Italian Morning Eggs, 163
Italian Sausage Frittata, 213
Italian Zucchini Frittata, 185
Joshua Grindle Inn, 7
Joshua Tree Inn Bed & Breakfast, 101
J. Patrick House Bed & Breakfast, 41
The Julian White House Bed &
    Breakfast, 253
Kristalberg Bed & Breakfast, 251

L

La Belle Grapes with Rosemary, 223
La chaumière, a country inn . . . ., 213
Lavender Hill Bed & Breakfast, 187
Lemons
    Lemon Curd, 239
    Lemon-Poppy Seed French Toast, 153
    Mini Lemon Muffins, 19
    Tart Lemon Tea Bread, 49
Lemon Curd, 239
Lemon-Poppy Seed French Toast, 153
Loma Vista Bed & Breakfast, 173
Lost Whale Inn, 119
Low-Fat Pineapple Bread, 51

M

Madison Street Inn, 165
Madrona Manor, 243
Mandarin Orange Muffins, 29
Maple syrup
    Decadent French Toast Soufflé, 105
    Lemon-Poppy Seed French Toast, 153
    Pineapple French Toast, 155
    Poached Pears in Raspberry Sauce, 231
    Portuguese French Toast, 157
Maricela's Salsa, 243
Mayan Maize Tortilla Pie, 183
Mayfield House Bed & Breakfast, 157
McCloud River Inn, 123
Meadow Creek Ranch Bed &
    Breakfast, 19
Melitta Station Inn, 107
Mendocino Village Inn, 37
Mesa Verde Plantation Bed &
    Breakfast, 79
Mimosa Truffles, 115
Mini Cake Doughnut Muffins, 33
Mini Cheese Soufflés, 179
Mini Lemon Muffins, 19
Mock Eggs Benedict, 173
Monterey jack cheese
    Baked Sour Cream Omelet, 211
    Cheesy Potato Pie, 201
    Chiles Rellenos, 167
    Cornmeal Soufflé, 181
    Crab Soufflé, 177
    Eye-Opener Jalapeño Corn Bread, 37
    Green Chile and Potato Tart, 195
    Ham and Cheese Breakfast Pie, 193
    Hash Brown Quiche, 187
    Italian Sausage Frittata, 213
    Sonoma County Egg Casserole, 209
    Vegetarian Breakfast Quiche, 191
Morning Baked Apples, 233
Muesli. *See* Granola

Muffins
    Apple-Cranberry Muffins, 25
    Apricot Cornmeal Muffins, 23
    Cran-Blackberry Muffins, 31
    Gingerbread Muffins, 15
    Ginger-Pear Muffins, 21
    Mandarin Orange Muffins, 29
    Mini Cake Doughnut Muffins, 33
    Mini Lemon Muffins, 19
    Pumpkin Pie Muffins, 27
    Super Cinnamon Muffins, 17
Murphy's Inn, 93
Mushrooms
    Artichoke-Mushroom Strata, 207
    Italian Sausage Frittata, 213
    Spinach Mushroom Quiche, 189
    Vegetarian Breakfast Quiche, 191

N–O

North Coast Country Inn, 171
Oatmeal and Cranberry Soufflé, 103
Oatmeal Buttermilk Pancakes, 119
Oatmeal Scones, 13
Oats
    Apple Oatmeal Crisp, 83
    Baked Banana Crumble, 225
    Breakfast Muesli, 77
    Cornmeal and Oat Waffles, 139
    Crunchy Nut Granola, 79
    Homestead Granola, 81
    Oatmeal and Cranberry Soufflé, 103
    Oatmeal Buttermilk Pancakes, 119
    Oatmeal Scones, 13
Old Monterey Inn, 207
Old Thyme Inn, 69
Oranges
    Baked Banana Crumble, 225
    Cheese Blintz Soufflé, 107
    Cherry Orange Scones, 9
    Gala Orange Sauce, 237
    Mandarin Orange Muffins, 29
    Morning Baked Apples, 233
    Oatmeal and Cranberry Soufflé, 103

    Orange Thyme Pancakes, 129
    Rosemary-Roasted Potatoes, 253
    Sunday's Baked French Toast, 151
    Warm Berry Sauce, 235
    White Fruit Cake, 73
Orange Thyme Pancakes, 129
Orchard Hill Country Inn, 29

P

The Palm Hotel Bed & Breakfast, 71
Pancakes
    Apfel Pfannkuchen, 131
    Apple Oven-Baked Pancake, 133
    Apple Walnut Pancakes, 127
    Fluffy Blueberry Pancakes, 121
    German Apple Pancakes, 123
    German Potato Pancakes, 251
    Oatmeal Buttermilk Pancakes, 119
    Orange Thyme Pancakes, 129
    Pear Dutch Baby, 89
    Ricotta Pancakes, 125
    See also Crepes
Parmesan cheese
    Artichoke Frittata, 215
    Baked Breakfast Polenta, 247
    Baked Sour Cream Omelet, 211
    Italian Morning Eggs, 163
    Italian Zucchini Frittata, 185
    Mock Eggs Benedict, 173
Peaches
    Hazelnut Waffles with Peaches, 137
    Peach-Stuffed French Toast, 149
    Peaches and Cream, 229
    Portuguese French Toast, 157
    Seasonal Fruit Crepes, 135
Peaches and Cream, 229
Peach-Stuffed French Toast, 149
Pear Dutch Baby, 89
Pears
    Ginger-Pear Muffins, 21
    Pear Dutch Baby, 89
    Poached Pears In Raspberry
        Sauce, 231

Pecan Pumpkin Bread, 45
Pecans
    Apple-Pecan French Toast, 159
    Caramel Apple French Toast, 147
    Crunchy Nut Granola, 79
    Date Pecan Scones, 11
    Decadent French Toast Soufflé, 105
    Fresh Fig Baked Custard, 97
    Gingerbread Muffins, 15
    Mandarin Orange Muffins, 29
    Oatmeal and Cranberry Soufflé, 103
    Pumpkin Pecan Bread, 45
    Pumpkin Pie Muffins, 27
    Sour Cream Coffee Cake, 57
    Super Cinnamon Muffins, 17
The Pelennor Bed & Breakfast, 179
Pelican Cove Inn, 149
The Philo Pottery Inn, 77
Pies
    Cheesy Potato Pie, 201
    Green Chile and Potato Tart, 195
    Ham and Cheese Breakfast Pie, 193
    Mayan Maize Tortilla Pie, 183
    Summer Plum Pie, 87
    See also Frittatas, Quiches
Pillar Point Inn, 201
Pineapple
    Hawaiian Bread, 43
    Low-Fat Pineapple Bread, 51
    Pineapple French Toast, 155
Pineapple French Toast, 155
Pine nuts
    Basil Tomatoes with Pine Nuts, 245
    Bella Torta, 199
    Crunchy Nut Granola, 79
Plum Coffee Cake, 69
Plums
    Plum Coffee Cake, 69
    Summer Plum Pie, 87
Poached Pears In Raspberry Sauce, 231
Portuguese French Toast, 157
Potatoes
    Ballard Home-Fried Potatoes, 255

Cheesy Potato Pie, 201
German Potato Pancakes, 251
Green Chile and Potato Tart, 195
Hash Brown Casserole, 219
Hash Brown Quiche, 187
Rosemary-Roasted Potatoes, 253
Provolone cheese
    Bella Torta, 199
Prufrock's Garden Inn, 39
Pumpkin
    Pecan Pumpkin Bread, 45
    Pumpkin Cranberry Coffee Cake, 55
    Pumpkin Pie Muffins, 27
    Pumpkin Spice Waffles, 141
Pumpkin Cranberry Coffee Cake, 55
Pumpkin Pie Muffins, 27
Pumpkin Spice Waffles, 141
Pudding
    Apple Pie Bread Pudding, 93
    Banana Nut Bread Pudding, 95
    Breakfast Berry Pudding, 91
    See also Custard

Q-R

Quiches
    Hash Brown Quiche, 187
    Spinach Mushroom Quiche, 189
    Vegetarian Breakfast Quiche, 191
    See also Frittatas, Pies
Rachel's Inn, 113
Raisins
    Apple-Cranberry Muffins, 25
    Applesauce Cake, 67
    Breakfast Muesli, 77
    Cinnamon-Glazed Scones, 5
    Cinnamon Raisin Breakfast
        Custard, 99
    Crunchy Nut Granola, 79
    Gingerbread Muffins, 15
    Ginger-Pear Muffins, 21
    Irish Soda Bread, 41
    Lemon-Poppy Seed French Toast, 153
    Oatmeal Scones, 13

Super Cinnamon Muffins, 17
White Fruit Cake, 73
Rancho San Gregorio, 185
Raspberries
    Breakfast Berry Pudding, 91
    Poached Pears in Raspberry Sauce, 231
    Raspberry Cream Cheese Coffee Cake,
    53
    Seasonal Fruit Crepes, 135
    Tart Lemon Tea Bread, 49
    Warm Berry Sauce, 235
Raspberry Cream Cheese Coffee Cake, 53
Rhubarb
    Fresh Rhubarb Cake, 71
Ricotta cheese
    Hash Brown Quiche, 187
    Ricotta Pancakes, 125
Ricotta Pancakes, 125
Rockwood Gardens Bed & Breakfast, 85
Rosemary
    La Belle Grapes with Rosemary, 223
    Rosemary-Roasted Potatoes, 253
Rosemary-Roasted Potatoes, 253
Rum Custard French Toast, 145
Ryan House, 1855, 73

S
Salsa
    Artichoke Frittata, 215
    Chiles Rellenos, 167
    Eggs Madison,
    165
    Maricela's Salsa, 243
Sauces
    Date-Nut Butter, 241
    Gala Orange Sauce, 237
    Lemon Curd, 239
    Maricela's Salsa, 243
    Warm Berry Sauce, 235
Sausage
    Italian Sausage Frittata, 213
    Sausage Strata, 205

Sausage with Grapes, 249
Sausage Strata, 205
Sausage with Grapes, 249
Scones
    Cherry Orange Scones, 9
    Cinnamon-Glazed Scones, 5
    Cranberry Buttermilk Scones, 7
    Date Pecan Scones, 11
    Oatmeal Scones, 13
Scott Courtyard, 153
Seasonal Fruit Crepes, 135
Serenity Bed & Breakfast Inn, 87
The Shore House at Lake Tahoe, 219
Side dishes
    Baked Breakfast Polenta, 247
    Ballard Home-Fried Potatoes, 255
    Basil Tomatoes with Pine Nuts, 245
    German Potato Pancakes, 251
    Rosemary-Roasted Potatoes, 253
    Sausage with Grapes, 249
Silver Rose Inn & Spa, 43
Simpson House Inn, 239
Sonoma County Egg Casserole, 209
Soufflés
    Cheese Blintz Soufflé, 107
    Cornmeal Soufflé, 181
    Crab Soufflé, 177
    Decadent French Toast Soufflé, 105
    Mini Cheese Soufflés, 179
    Oatmeal and Cranberry Soufflé, 103
Sour cream
    Artichoke Frittata, 215
    Baked Sour Cream Omelet, 211
    Blueberry Cream Cheese Coffee
    Cake, 65
    Broiled Blackberries, 227
    Cheese Blintz Soufflé, 107
    Chiles Rellenos, 167
    Cottage Cheese Blintz, 101
    Crab Soufflé, 177
    Creamy Eggs with Caviar, 171
    Eggs Madison, 165
    Gingerbread Muffins, 15

Irish Soda Bread, 41
La Belle Grapes with Rosemary, 223
Mandarin Orange Muffins, 29
Pineapple French Toast, 155
Raspberry Cream Cheese Coffee Cake,
   53
Sour Cream Coffee Cake, 57
Tart Lemon Tea Bread, 49
Sour Cream Coffee Cake, 57
Spiced Banana Cake, 61
Spinach
   Italian Morning Eggs, 163
   Spinach Mushroom Quiche, 189
Spinach Mushroom Quiche, 189
The Stanford Inn by the Sea, 195
Strawberries
   Strawberry Nut Bread, 47
   Warm Berry Sauce, 235
Strawberry Creek Inn, 211
Strawberry Nut Bread, 47
Summer Plum Pie, 87
Sunday's Baked French Toast, 151
Sun-dried tomatoes
   Bella Torta, 199
   Hash Brown Casserole, 219
   Italian Morning Eggs, 163
Super Cinnamon Muffins, 17
Sutter Creek Inn, 83
The Swedish House Bed & Breakfast, 133
Swiss cheese
   Artichoke-Mushroom Strata, 207
   Baked Breakfast Polenta, 247
   Mock Eggs Benedict, 173
   Spinach Mushroom Quiche, 189

T

Tart Lemon Tea Bread, 49
Tiffany House Bed & Breakfast, 227
Todd Farm House Bed & Breakfast, 189
Tomatoes
   Basil Tomatoes with Pine Nuts, 245
   Cornmeal Soufflé, 181

Eggs Gruyère with Savory Garnish,
   217
Ham and Cheese Breakfast Pie, 193
Maricela's Salsa, 243
Victorian Eggs, 175
Tres Palmas Bed & Breakfast, 33

U–W

Vegetarian Breakfast Quiche, 191
Vichy Hot Springs Resort & Inn, 59
Victorian Eggs, 175
Vineyard Country Inn, 45
Waffles
   Cornmeal and Oat Waffles, 139
   Hazelnut Waffles with Peaches, 137
   Pumpkin Spice Waffles, 141
   Whole Wheat Belgian Waffles, 143
Walnuts
   Apple Walnut Pancakes, 127
   Applesauce Cake, 67
   Banana Nut Bread Pudding, 95
   Blueberry Cream Cheese Coffee
      Cake, 65
   Chocolate Zucchini Rum Cake, 63
   Cottage Cheese Blintz, 101
   Date-Nut Butter, 241
   Espresso Biscotti, 111
   Fresh Fig Baked Custard, 97
   Fresh Rhubarb Cake, 71
   Ginger-Pear Muffins, 21
   Oatmeal and Cranberry Soufflé, 103
   Plum Coffee Cake, 69
   Pumpkin Pie Muffins, 27
   Spiced Banana Cake, 61
   Strawberry Nut Bread, 47
   Super Cinnamon Muffins, 17
   Walnut Shortbread, 113
Walnut Shortbread, 113
Warm Berry Sauce, 235
A Weaver's Inn, 229
The Wedgewood Inn, 245
The Whale Watch Inn, 99

White Fruit Cake, 73
Whitegate Inn Bed & Breakfast, 147
White Horse Inn Bed & Breakfast, 121
Whole Wheat Belgian Waffles, 143

X-Z
Yogurt
    Fluffy Blueberry Pancakes, 121
    Hazelnut Waffles with Peaches, 137

Herbed Baked Eggs, 169
Seasonal Fruit Crepes, 135
Whole Wheat Belgian Waffles, 143
The Yosemite Peregrine Bed &
Breakfast, 103
The Zaballa House Bed & Breakfast, 33
Zucchini
    Chocolate Zucchini Rum Cake, 63
    Italian Zucchini Frittata, 185

SCOTT WYBERG

About the Author

Carol Frieberg is the author of the best-selling Northwest *Breakfast in Bed Cookbook*. Currently a food editor, she holds a degree in Home Economics Education from the University of Wisconsin, Madison. She has been active in the food and nutrition field for fifteen years. A native of the Midwest, Frieberg managed two bed-and-breakfast inns in Door County, Wisconsin, where she cooked both hearty country breakfasts and full-course weekend meals. She has traveled to many B&Bs across the country and loves to gather new recipes.